Niagara-on-the-Lake Ontario Book 1 in Colour Photos, Saving Our History One Photo at a Time

Photography
by Barbara Raué
2015

Series Name:
Cruising Ontario

Book 102: Niagara-on-the-Lake Book 1

Cover photo: The Prince of Wales Hotel

Series Name: Cruising Ontario
Saving Our History One Photo at a Time
in colour photos

Other Books by Barbara Raue

Coins of Gold

Arrows, Indians and Love

The Life and Times of Barbara
Volume 1: Inventions That Have Enhanced My Life
Volume 2: Entertainment That I Have Enjoyed
Volume 3: East Coast Trips
Volume 4: Olympics Have Always Intrigued Me
Volume 5: Wonders of the World
Volume 6: Caribbean Cruises We Have Enjoyed
Volume 7: Animals
Volume 8: Storms and Other Major Disasters in My Lifetime
Volume 9: Wars, Terrorist Attacks and Major Disasters

The Cromwell Family Book

Laura Secord Discovered

Daddy Where Are You?

Visit Barbara's website to view all of her books
http://barbararaue.ca

Known at various times as Butlersburg, West Niagara, and Newark, its first permanent settlers, Butler's Rangers and other Loyalist refugees arrived in 1778 when they began crossing from Fort Niagara to settle the west bank of the Niagara River. A town was laid out in a grid pattern of four-acre blocks and grew quickly, gaining prominence as the first capital of Upper Canada from 1792 to 1796. The town was captured by American forces on May 27, 1813; upon their withdrawal on December 13, 1813, the American forces burned the town.

Following Niagara's destruction, the citizens rebuilt mainly in the British classical architectural tradition, creating a group of structures closely related in design, material and scale. Spared from redevelopment, the town's colonial buildings eventually became one of its greatest resources. Beginning in the 1950s, residents rehabilitated and restored old structures, demonstrating an exceptional commitment to the preservation of local heritage.

The Prince of Wales Hotel is a historic Victorian hotel located at King Street and Picton Street. Built in 1864, the three storey 110 room hotel went by several names (Long's Hotel, Arcade Hotel, The Niagara House) and was renamed with the current name after famous guests The Duke of York (and Prince of Wales) and The Duchess of York in 1901. Queen Elizabeth II stayed at the hotel during her visit to the area in 1973.

Table of Contents

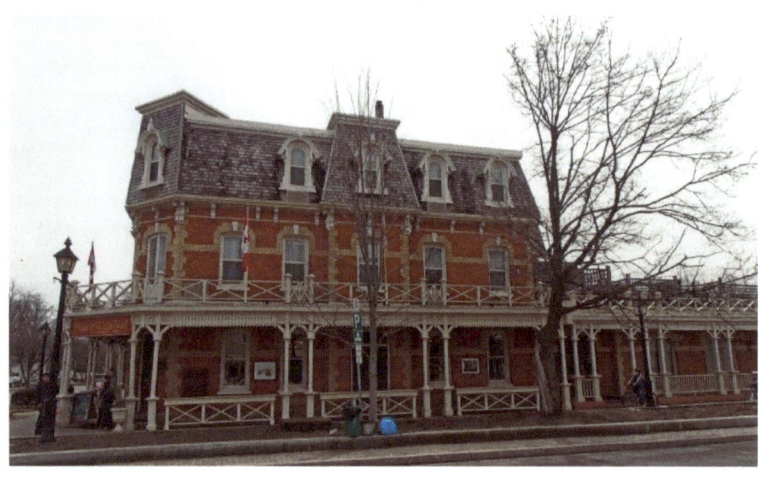

6 Picton Street – The Prince of Wales Hotel established 1864
Second Empire style, mansard roof, dormers, window hoods,
dichromatic brickwork, cornice brackets, second floor balcony

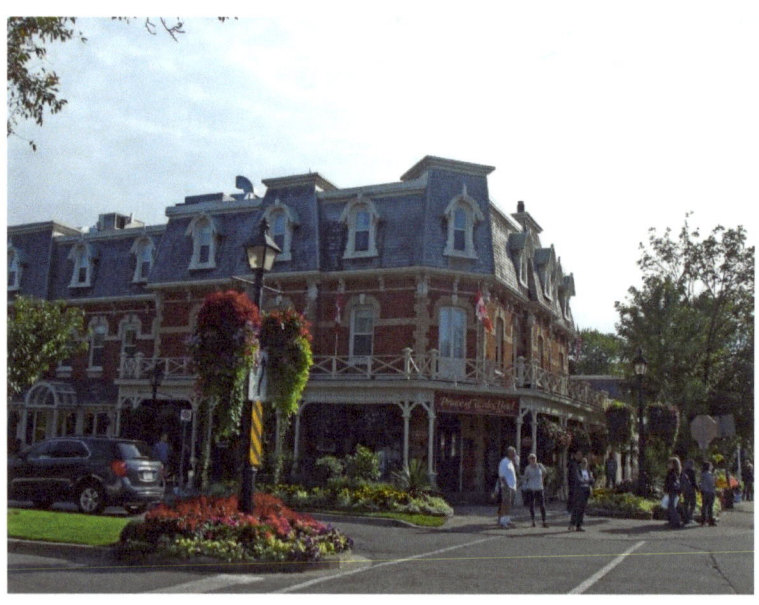

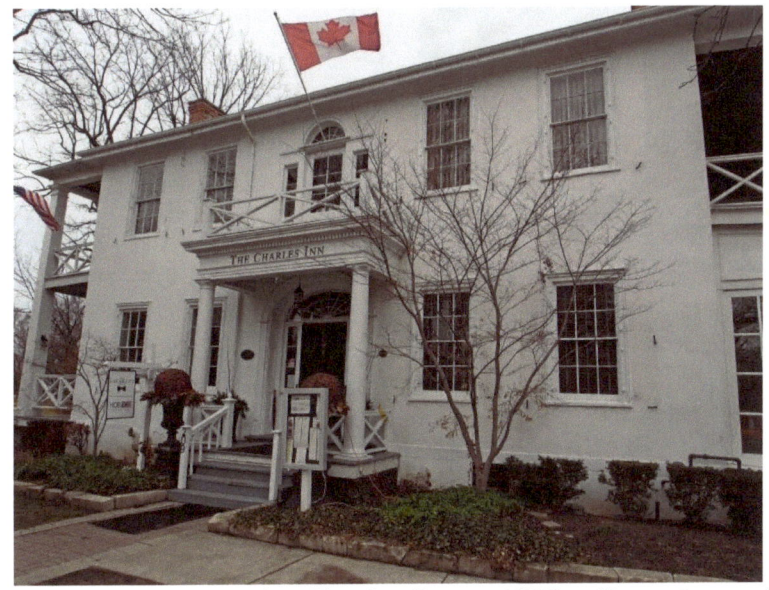

209 Queen Street - The Charles Inn c. 1832 – Georgian style

English Civil Law was introduced into this province in 1792. The Law Society of Upper Canada was established here in 1797 when ten practitioners met at Wilson's Hotel for the founding meeting. The Society was responsible for setting standards for admission and regulating the province's legal profession. In the late eighteenth century, the Society relocated to York (now Toronto).

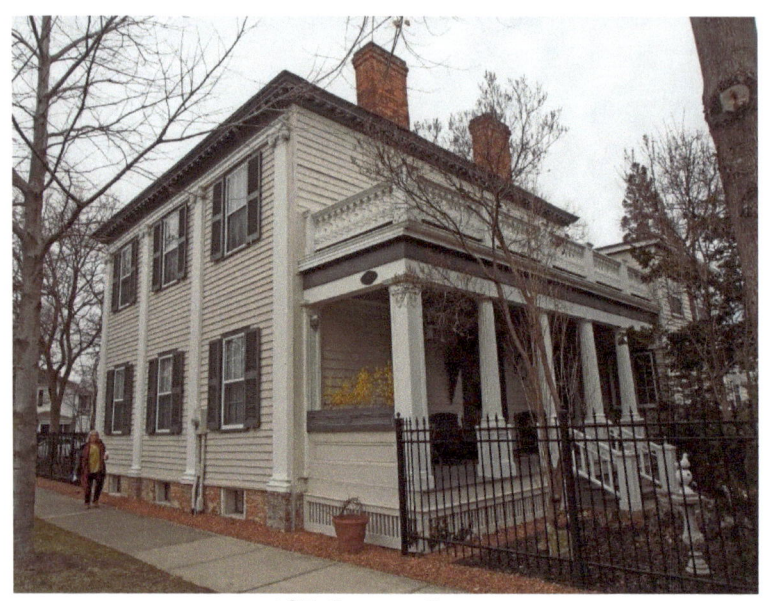

187 Queen Street

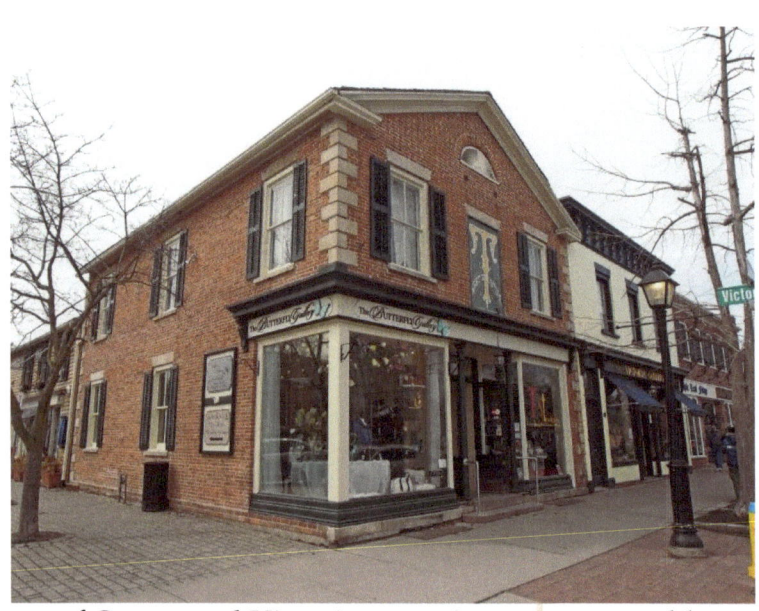

Corner of Queen and Victoria – cornice return on gable, corner
quoins

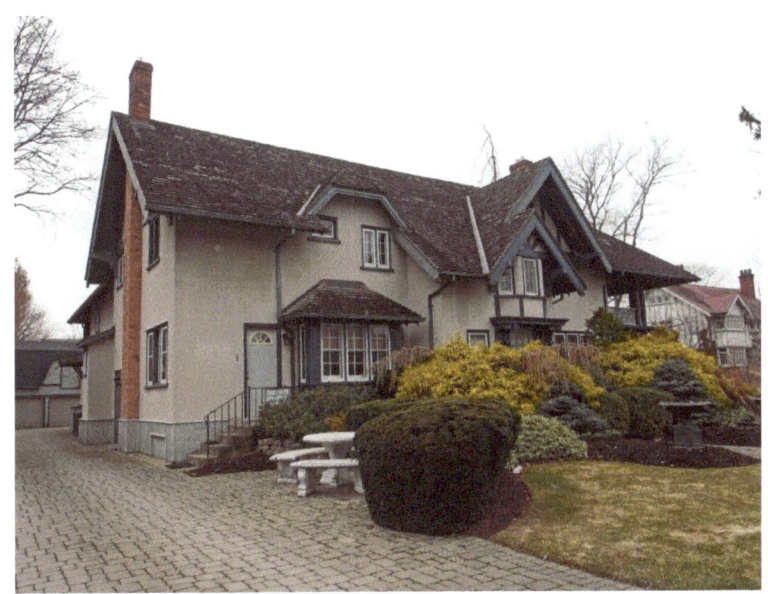

Queen Street – Gothic Revival

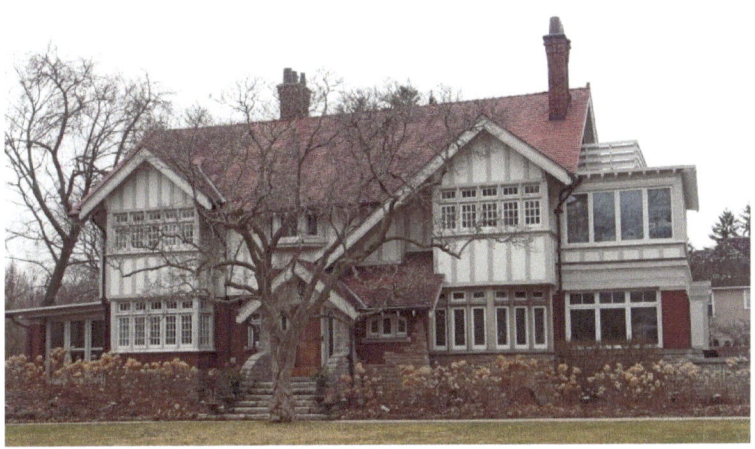

184 Queen Street – Tudor style

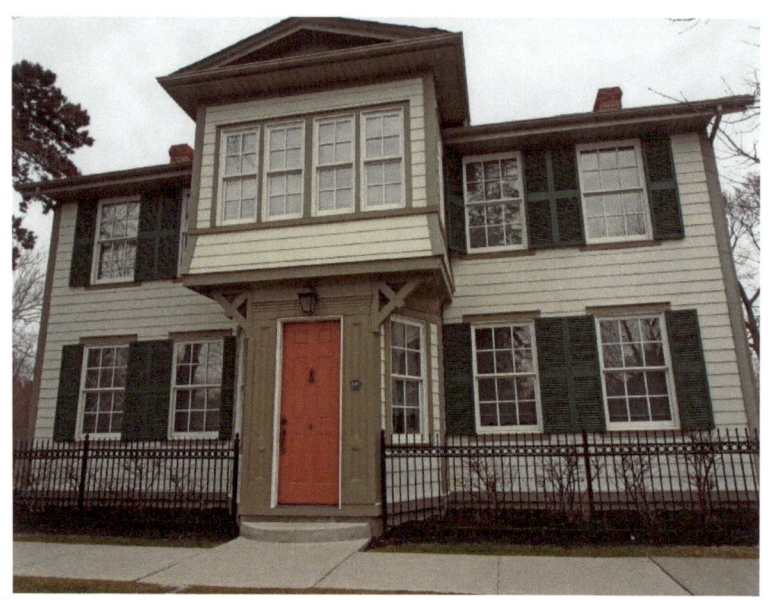

175 Queen Street – Georgian style with large dormer over entrance topped with pediment - c. 1820

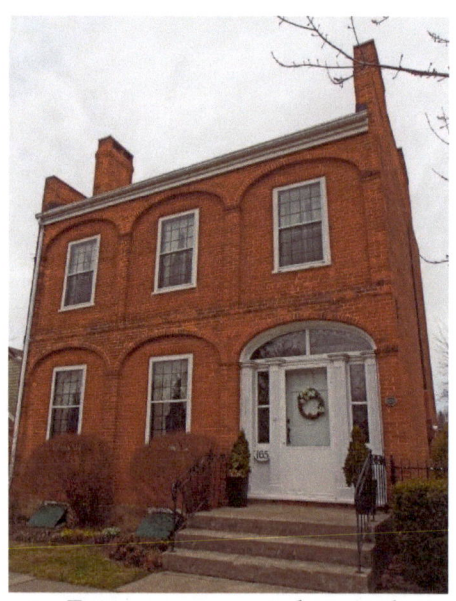

165 Queen Street – Romanesque style window voussoirs with pilasters, transom window and side lights – c. 1820

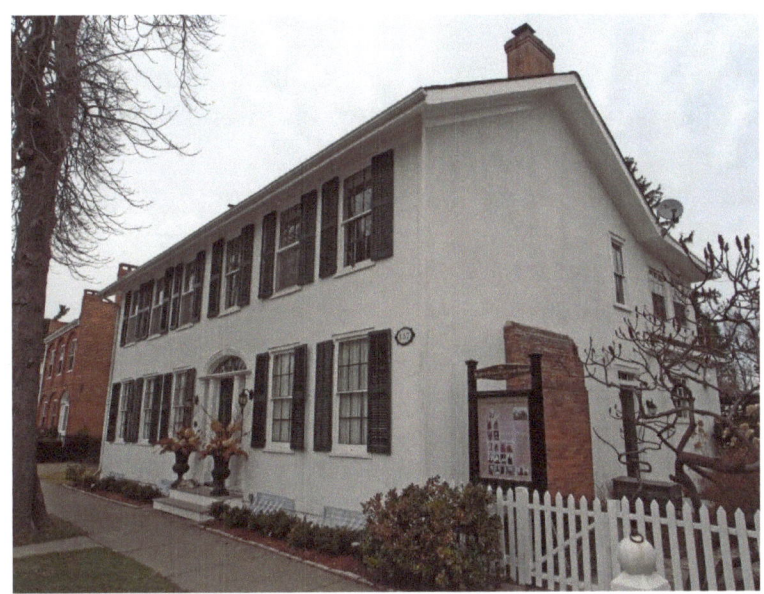

157 Queen Street - The Rogers-Blake-Harrison House c. 1817

John Rogers and his wife Mary arrived in Upper Canada's first capital in 1806 from County Cork, Ireland. They had four children: James, Alexander, Joseph and Mary.

On December 10, 1813, the retreating Americans burned the town. Alexander started rebuilding the home in 1817 and it was completed by his wife Agnes in 1823 when the final payment for war losses was received.

Alexander and Agnes Progress Ongony had four children: James, John, Margaret, and Mary Ann. Agnes was widowed in 1819 and she operated the family hotel, "Mrs. A. Rogers Inn," "The Sign of the Anchor & The Swan" during the 1820s and early 1830s.

Alexander and Agnes' son John became a very successful merchant. John's sister Mary Ann married a merchant, John Blake. John Blake and his brother-in-law John Rogers formed a company, "Rogers and Blake" and they built the town's largest building at the time, a three storey brick building attached to the family home.

John Blake died in 1835 and Mary Ann gave birth several months later to their second child, John Alexander Blake. Mary Ann lived with her two children (Agnes and John) with her mother in the family home.

By 1856 John had become a lieutenant in the local militia. He married Gertrude Smith Hakes and they settled in Port Robinson where John owned a mill. At the age of 24, Gertie, the mother of two small children, Ada and Herbert, died. The children were raised by John's mother Mary Ann and his grandmother Agnes in this home.

A few years later John married his wife's sister, Harriet Maria Smith and raised two daughters. Annie Maud Black, second daughter of John Alexander and his second wife Harriet, married William Henry Harrison from Indiana. Annie Maud was an accomplished organist at St. Andrew's Presbyterian Church.

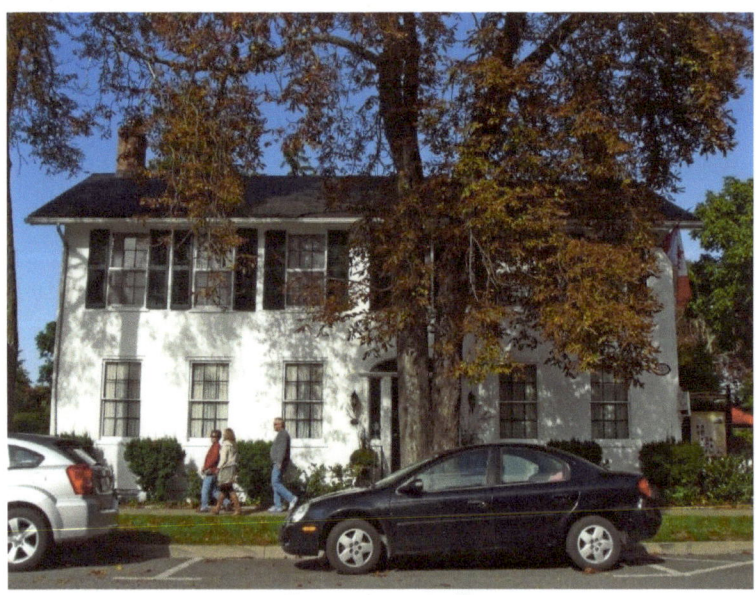

Georgian style

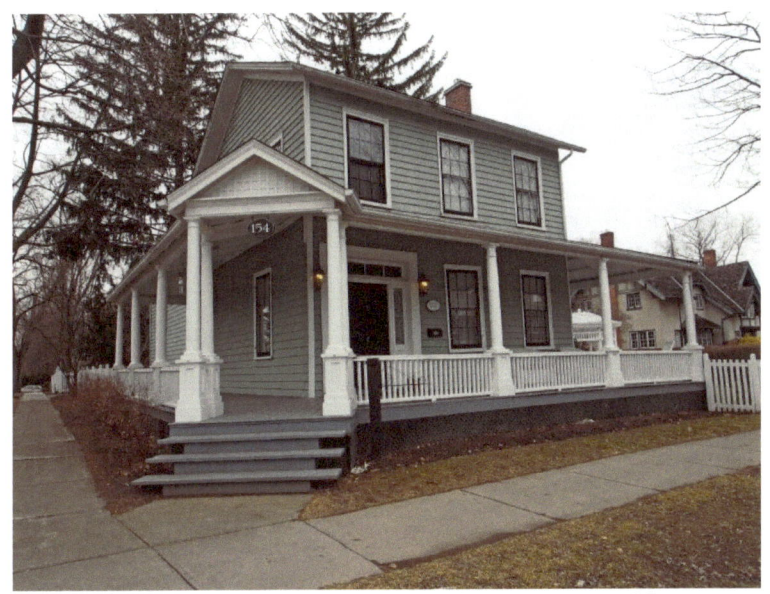

154 Queen Street – Doctor's House c. 1824
Pediment, board and batten construction

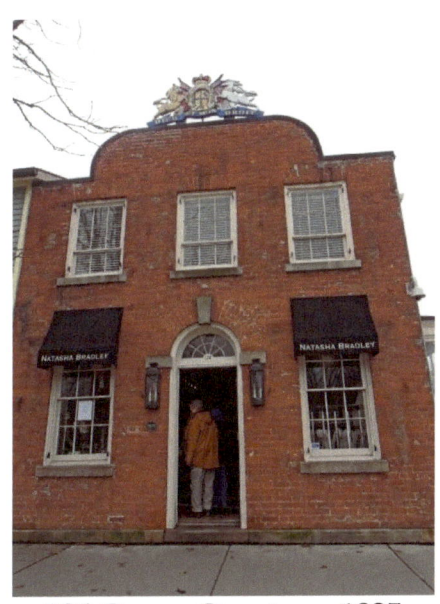

126 Queen Street – c. 1825

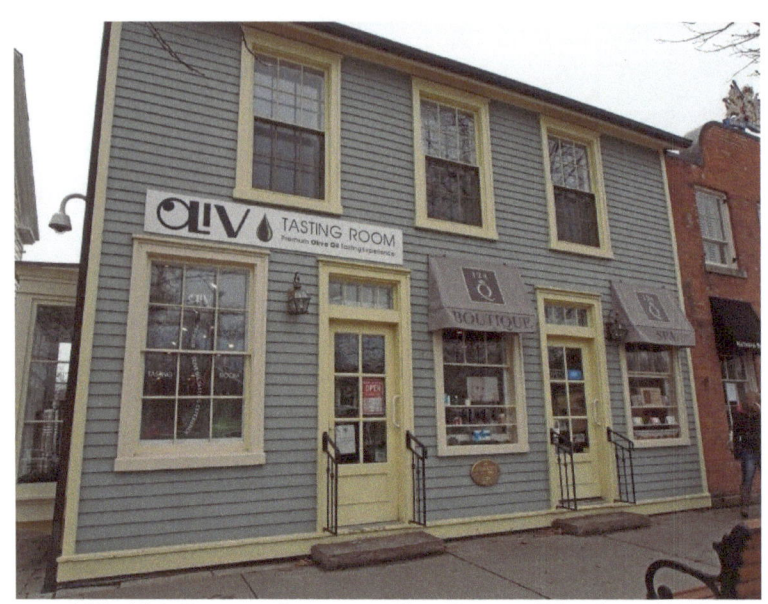

122-124 Queen Street – The Evans Block c. 1840

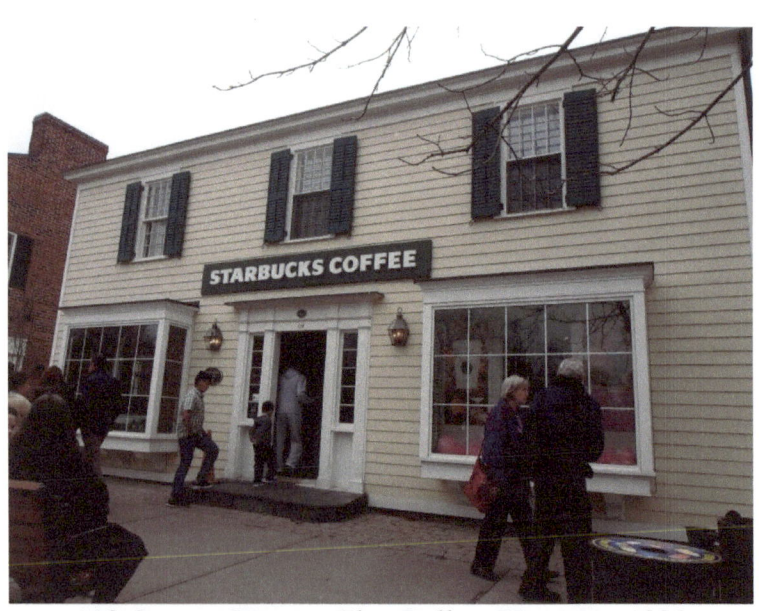

118 Queen Street – The Gollop House c. 1830

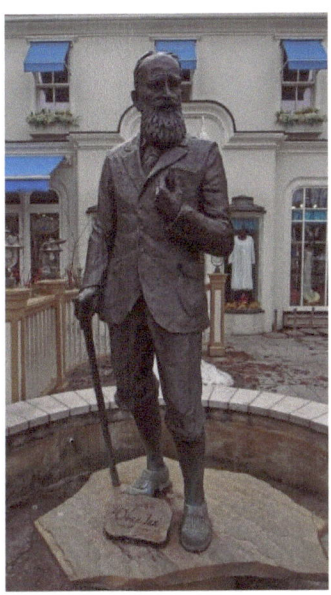

George Bernard Shaw (1856-1950) born in Dublin, Ireland
Noted spokesperson and playwright awarded Nobel Prize for
Literature 1925 (Elizabeth Bradford Holbrook, sculptor)

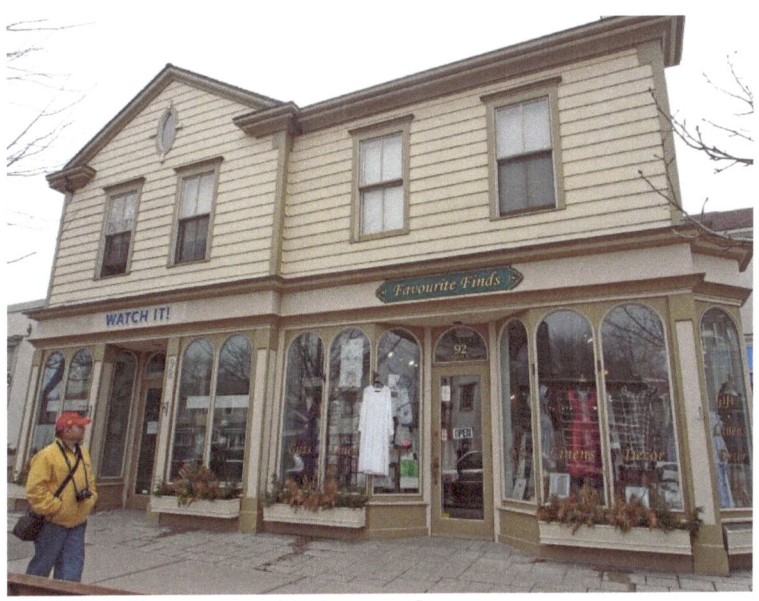

92 Queen Street

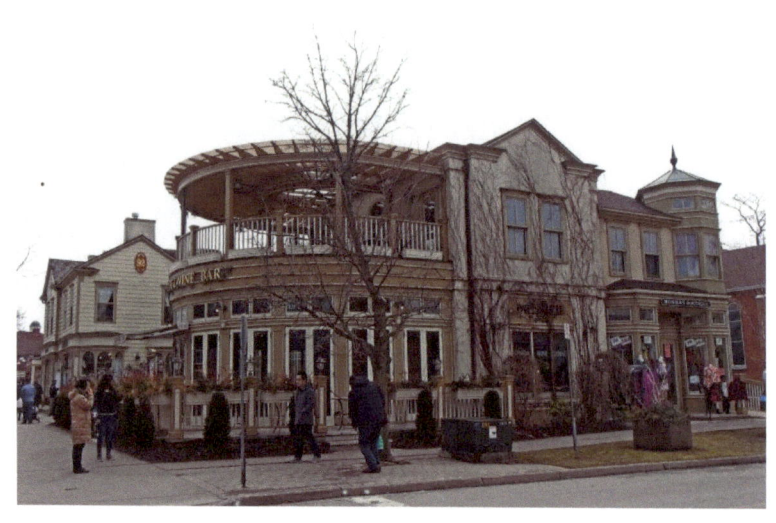

92 Queen Street

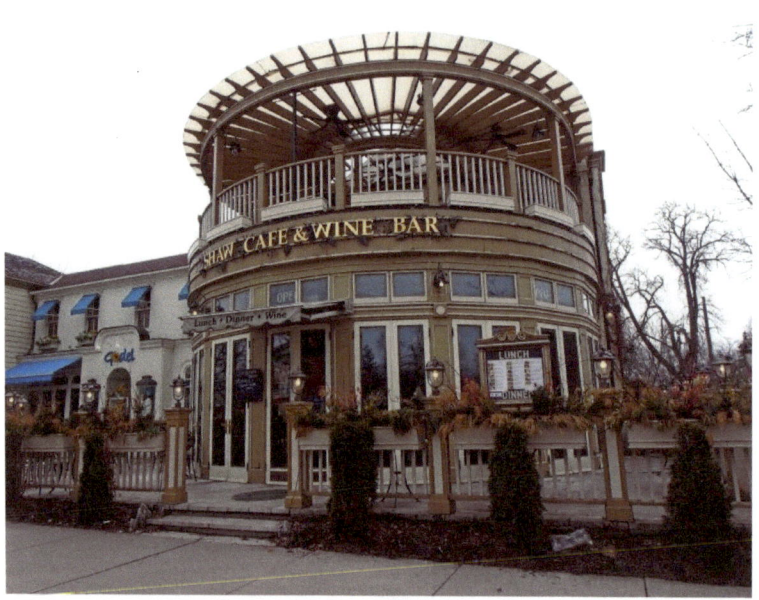

Shaw Café and Wine Bar

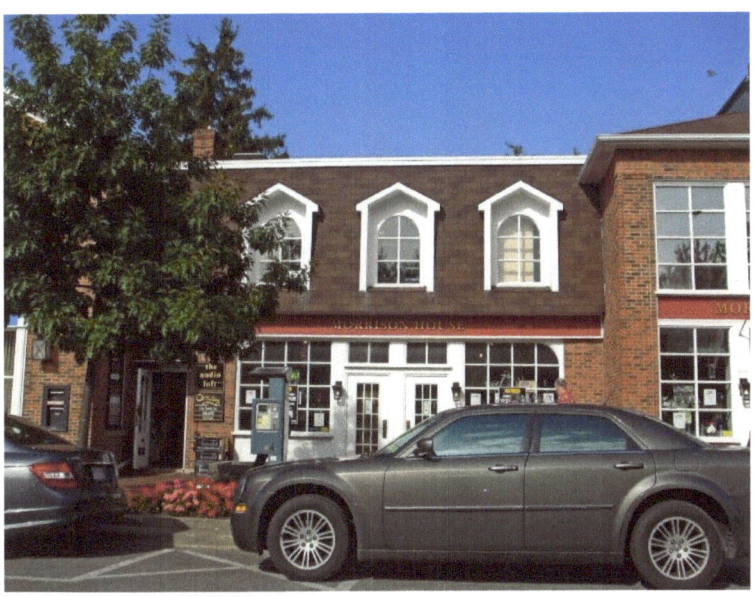

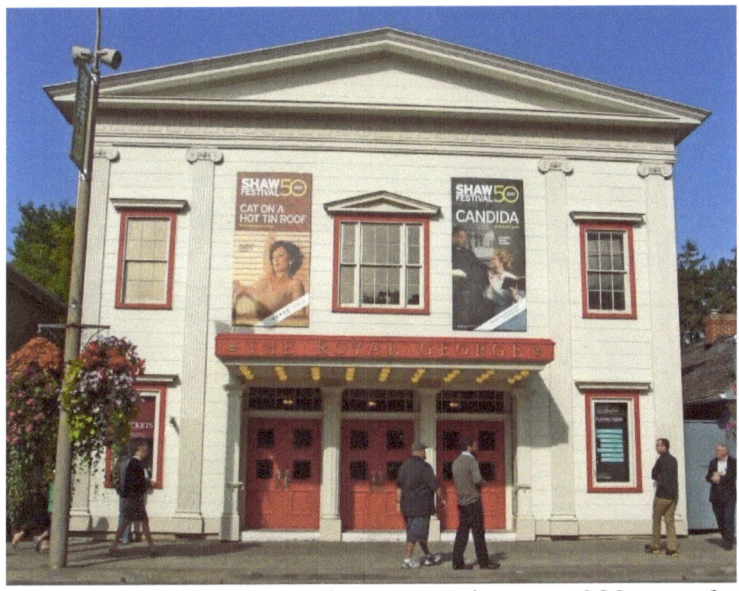

85 Queen Street – The Royal George Theatre - 328-seat theatre built as a vaudeville house to entertain troops during World War I

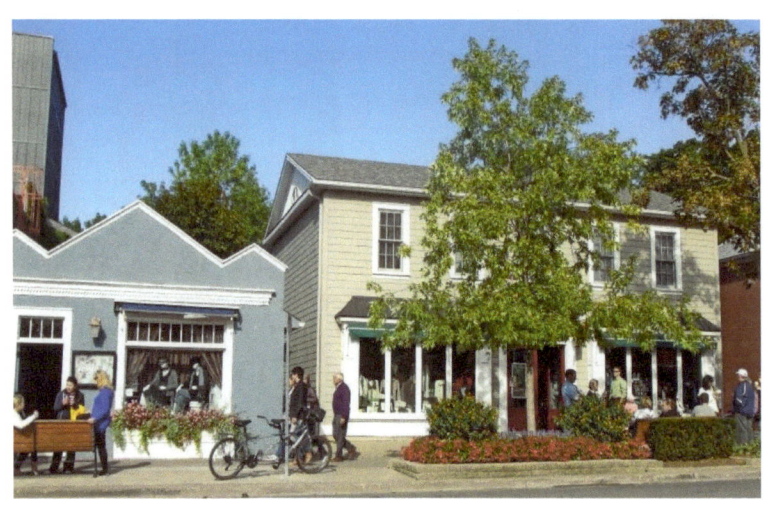

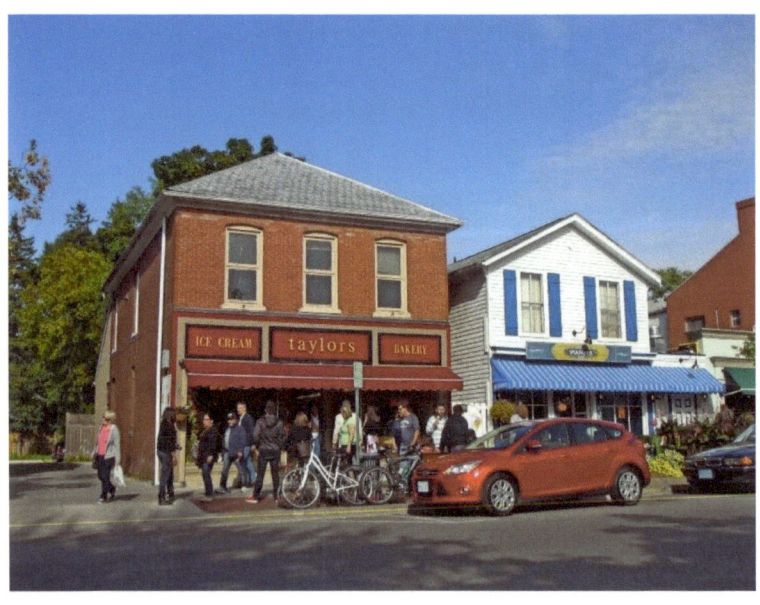

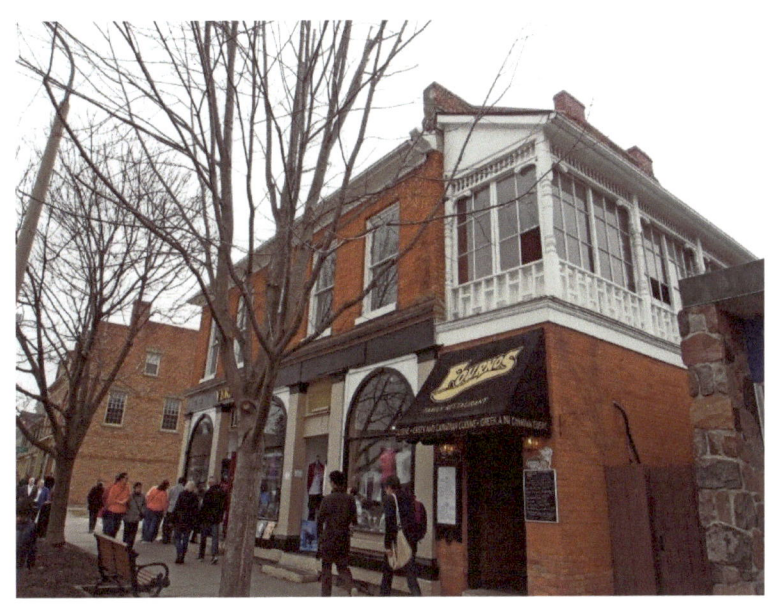

54-56 Queen Street

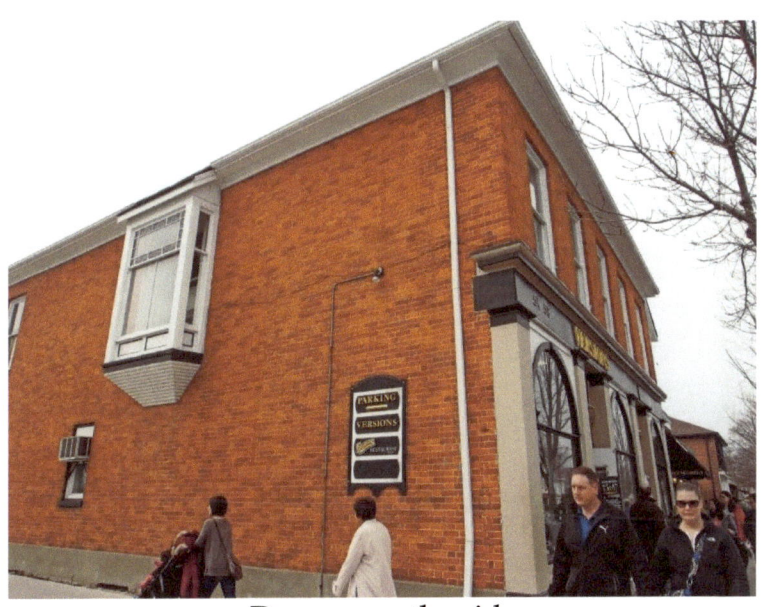

Dormer on the side

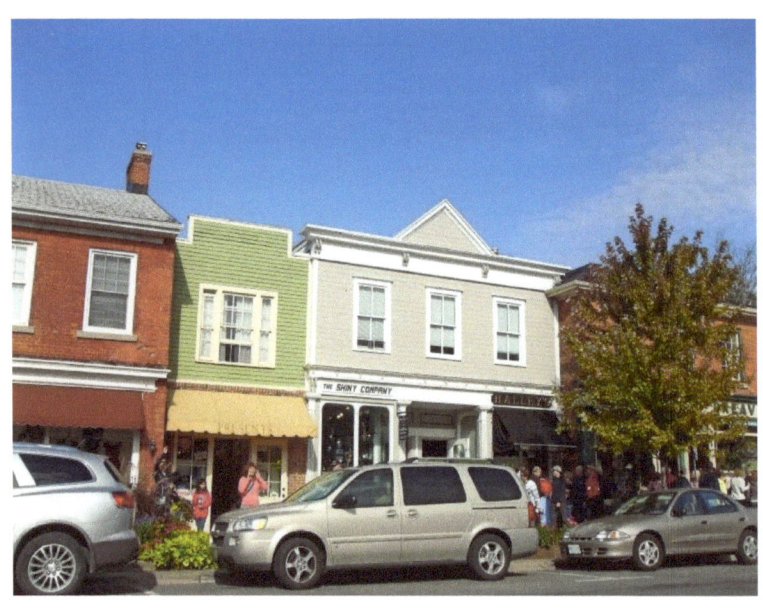

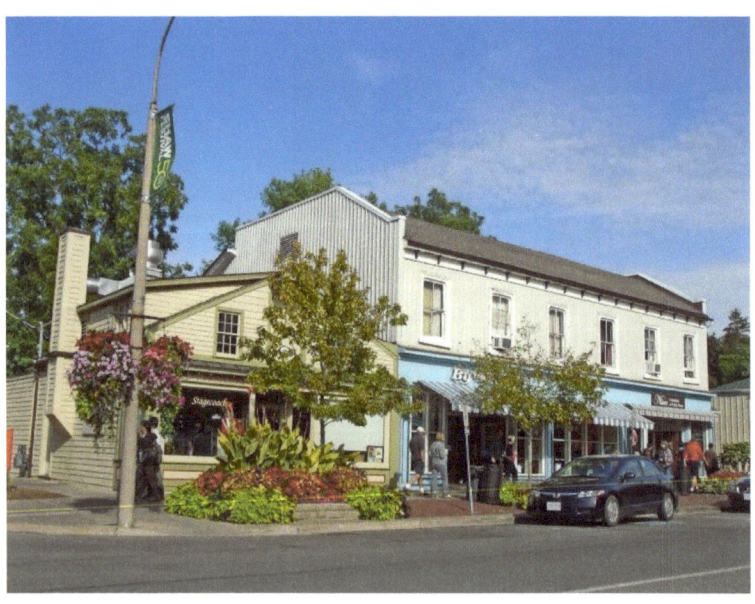

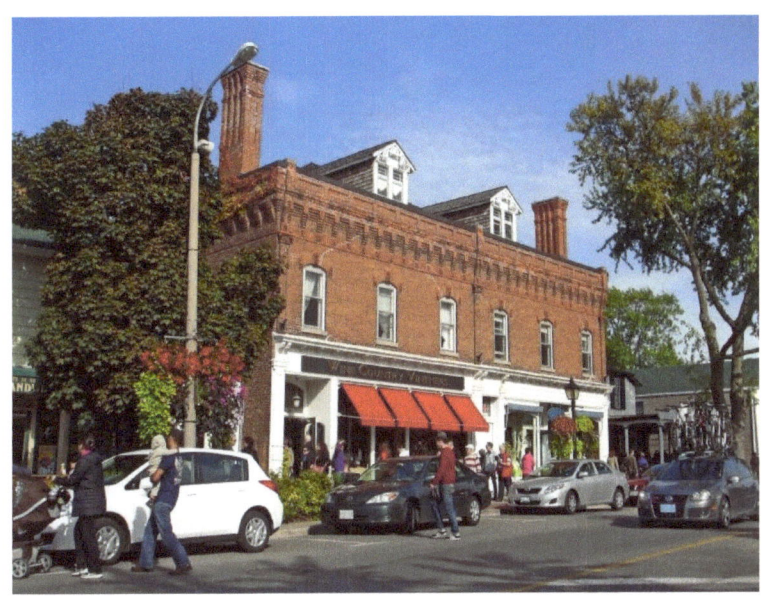

Bevelled dentil moulding, dormers on the roof, voussoirs and keystones

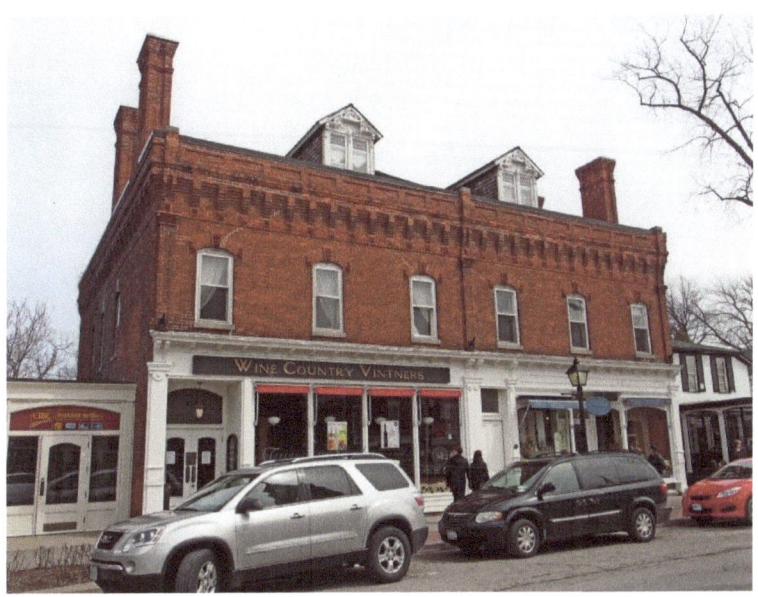

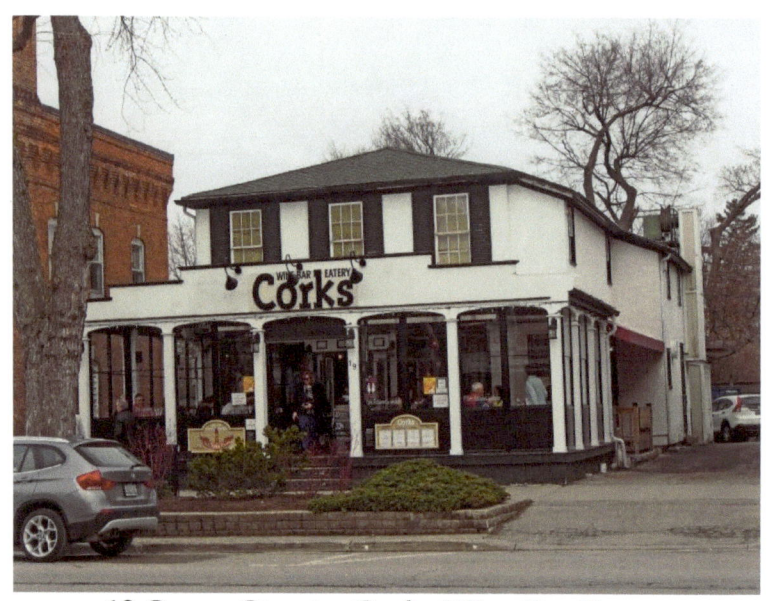

19 Queen Street – Corks Wine Bar Eatery
Hipped roof

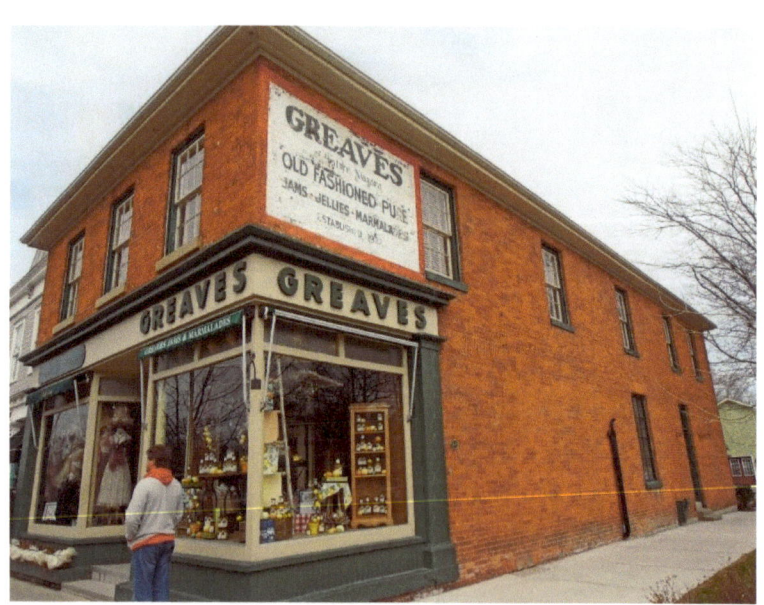

Queen Street c. 1845

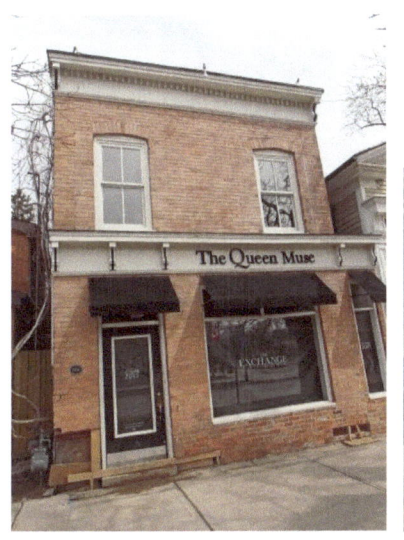

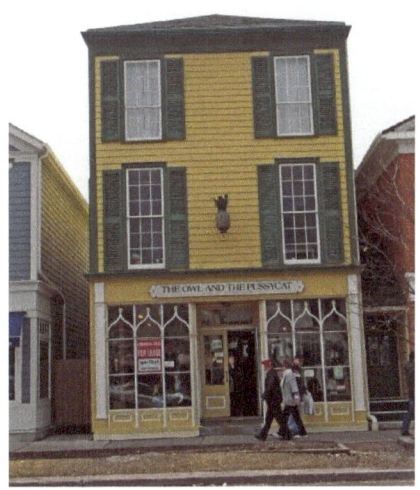

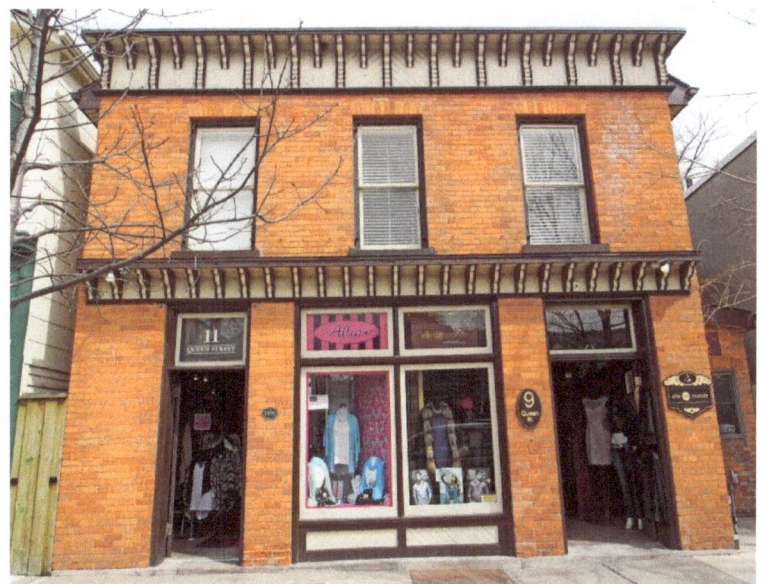

9 and 11 Queen Street – c. 1890 – cornice brackets

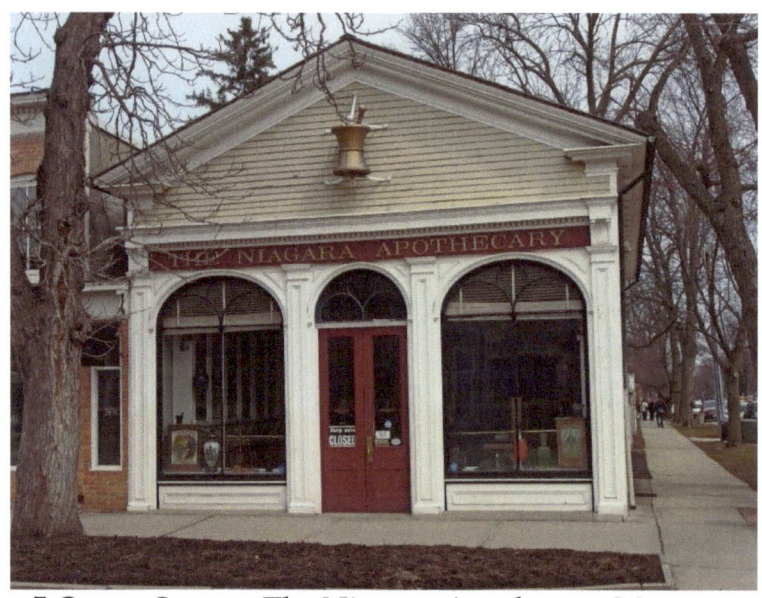

5 Queen Street – The Niagara Apothecary Museum
Cornice return on gable

It is a fine example of a Confederation era commercial establishment and pharmacy. It was built in the 1820s but extensively renovated in 1866 at which time the Italianate windows were installed and the interior was fitted up as a drug store. Until it closed in 1964, it was one of the oldest and one of the longest continuously operating pharmaceutical practices in Canada.

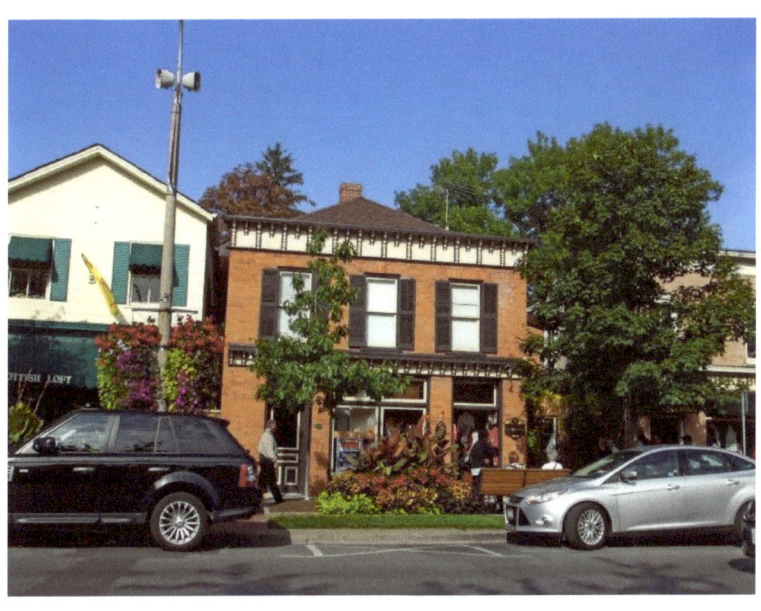

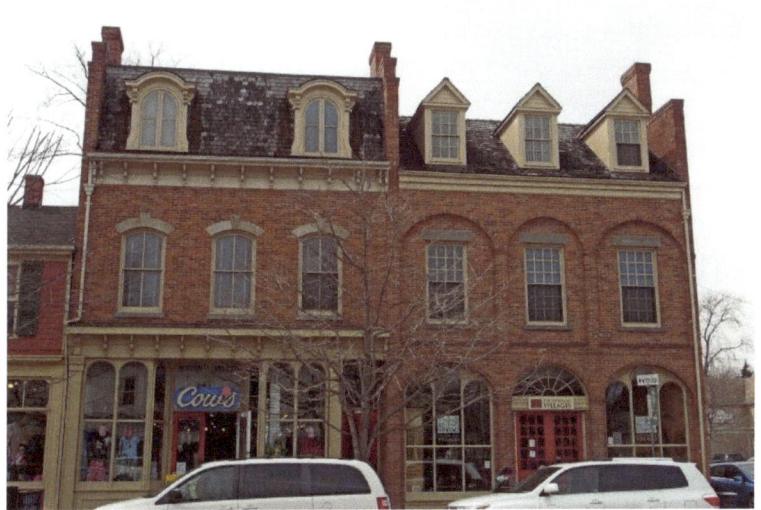

Queen Street – mansard roof on left, dormers with window hoods, cornice brackets, keystones above some windows

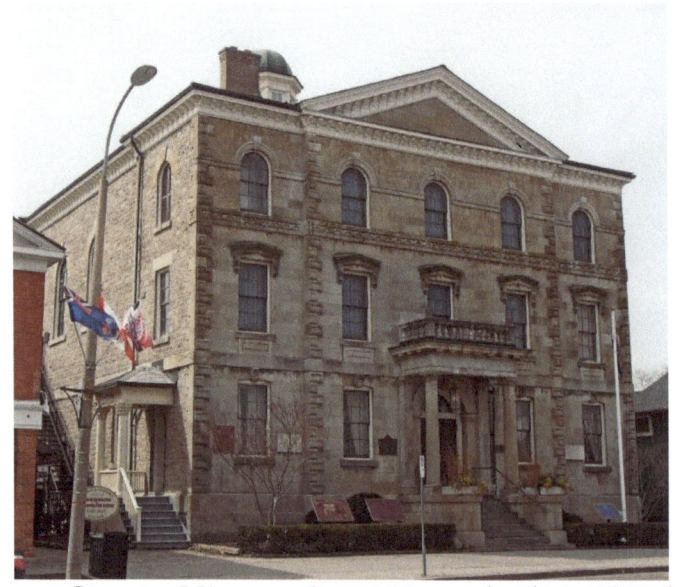

26 Queen Street – Niagara Court House built in 1847 for the united counties of Lincoln, Welland and Haldimand

This is the third and only surviving court house erected for the former Niagara district. Constructed between 1846 and 1848, it is in the Neo-classical style.

Though the courts were moved to St. Catharines in 1862, this building continued to play an important role in the life of the community. It served as the Town Hall and later as the founding home of the Shaw Festival.

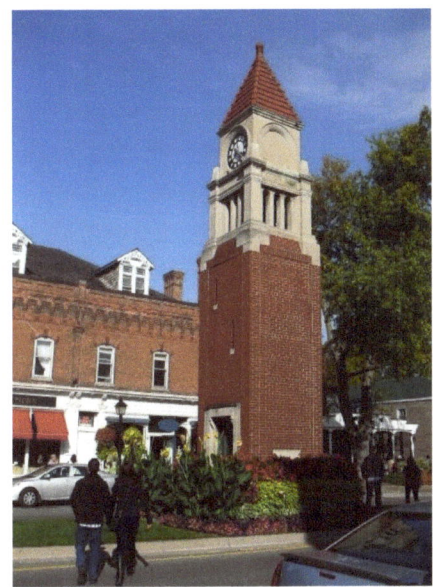
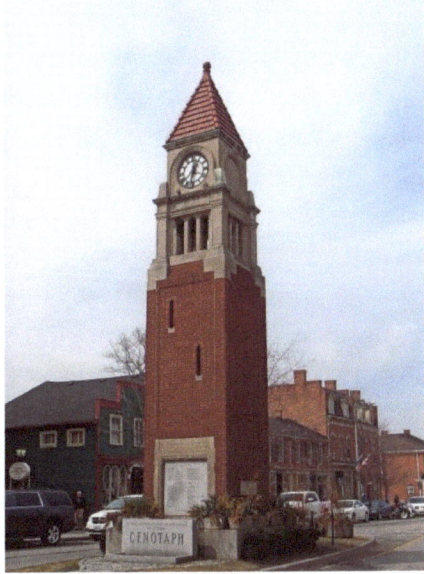

Queen Street - Cenotaph

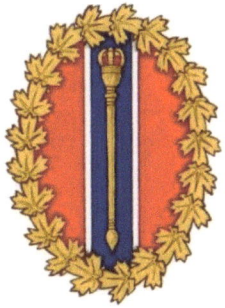

Badge - The maple leafs coronets indicate the town's Canadian
identity.

Coat of Arms – Brock's monument is an important local landmark commemorating the Battle of Queenston Heights in 1812. The green colour of the ribbons around the necks of the lions is associated with Butler's Rangers, who settled in the Niagara area following the American revolutionary War. Gorgets (a single piece of plate armour hanging from the neck serving as a symbolic accessory on military uniforms) were worn by British Army officers until 1830 and the one on the lion alludes to the regiment's leader, Colonel John Butler, the founder of the town. The other lion wears a medal as a reference the medals bearing the King's effigy given to First Nations chiefs in recognition of the support of the First Nations during the War of 1812 which helped to build a peaceful foundation in the area for the years to follow. The stylized water represents Lake Ontario and the Niagara River, and the base pays tribute to the importance of the local fruit and wine industries.

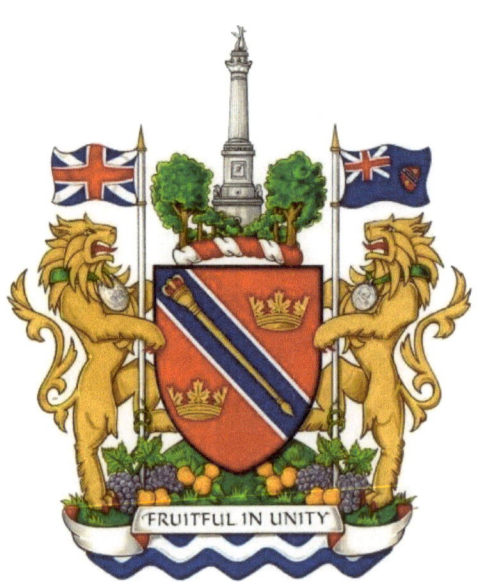

On December 10, 2013, 200 years after the burning of the town during the War of 1812 to 1814, the Town of Niagara unveiled its first Town flag. The flag is a symbol of new beginnings and a lasting legacy of peace between the British Crown and United States. It features the Royal Union Flag of 1707 and the shield from the Town's Official Coat of Arms granted by the Canadian Heraldic Authority. The mace within the shield is a gilt wood object dating from 1792 and indicates that Niagara-on-the-Lake, known then as Newark, was the first capital of the province of Upper Canada.

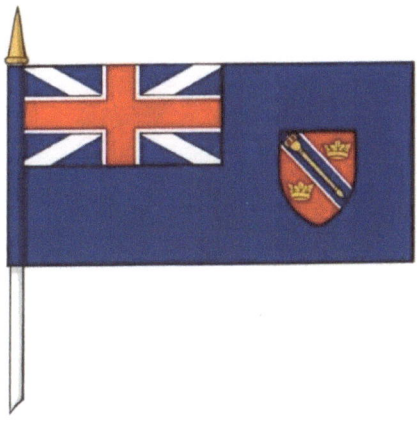

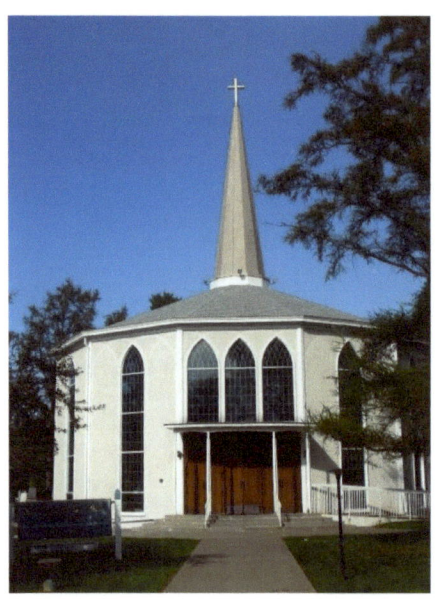

93 Picton Street – St. Vincent de Paul was established in 1827, evangelizing Natives and providing chaplains for the soldiers of Fort George and Fort Mississauga. In 1835, the church was erected and it is the oldest operational Catholic Church in Ontario. The polygon shaped addition to the front of the building was added in 1965.

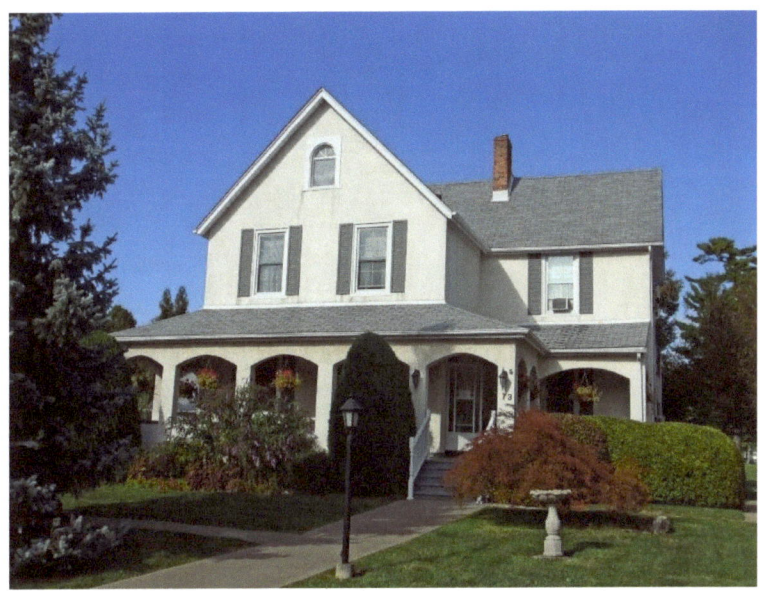

73 Picton Street – Gothic Revival

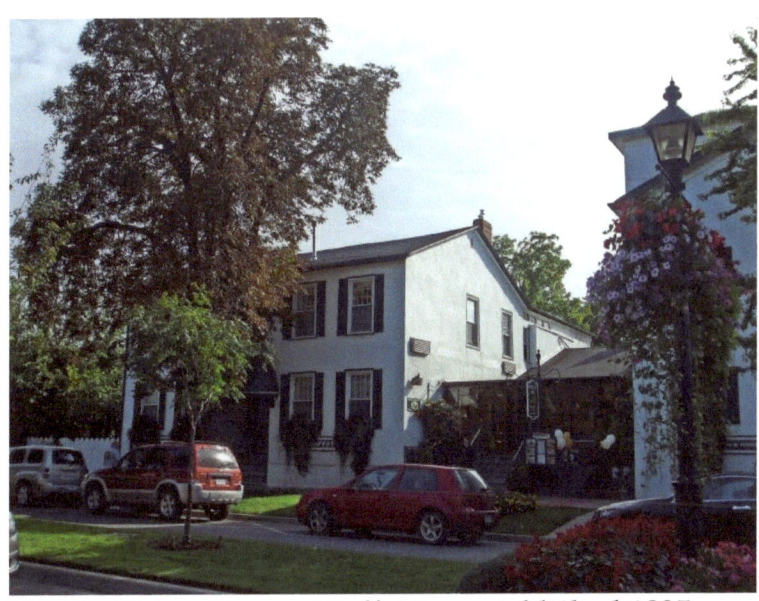

60 Picton Street - Moffat Inn established 1835

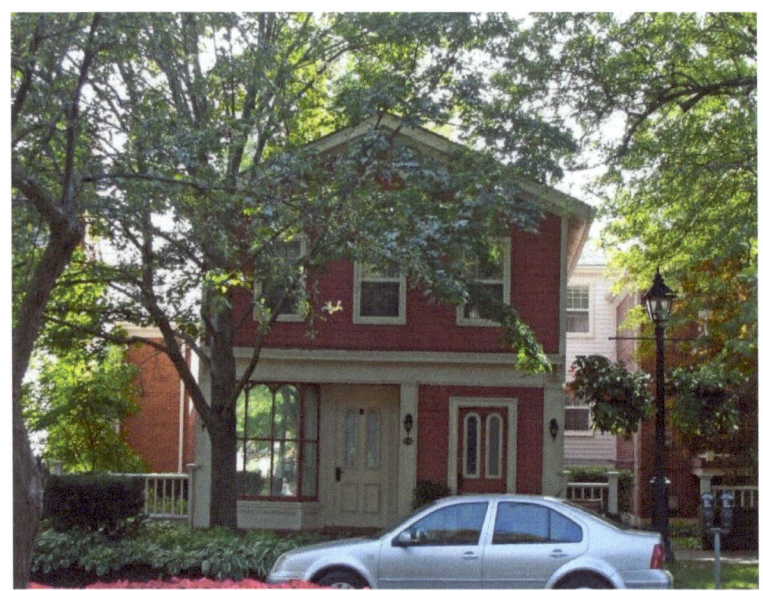

Picton Street

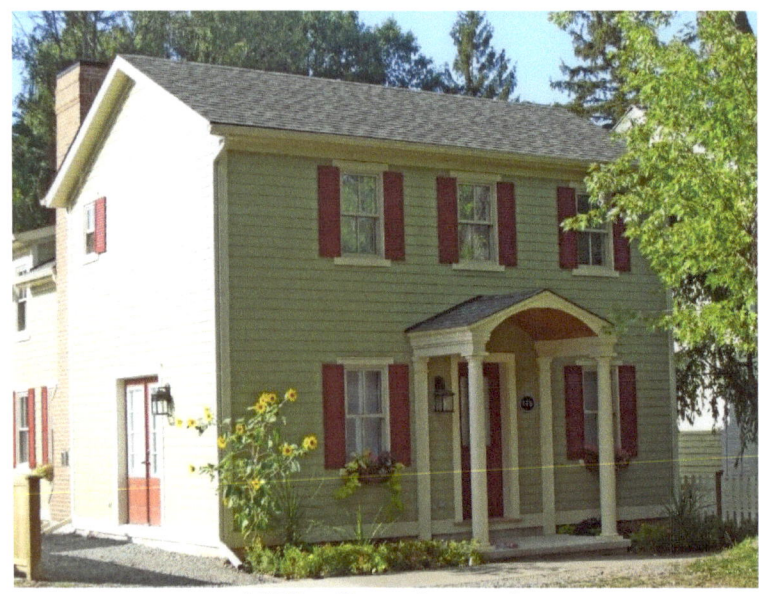

#179 – Georgian style

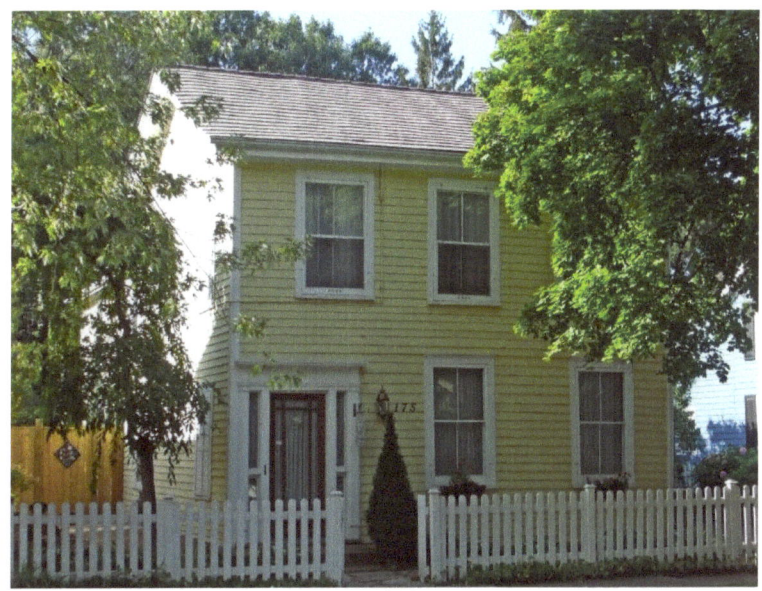

#175

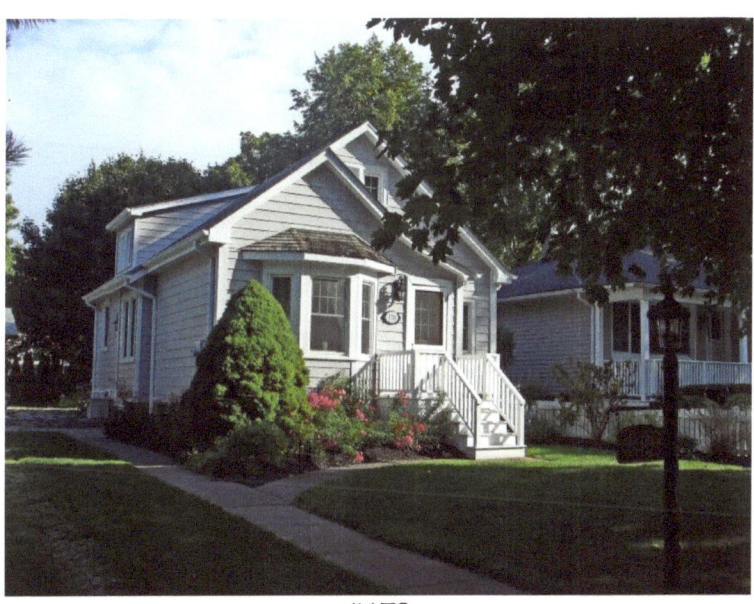

#178

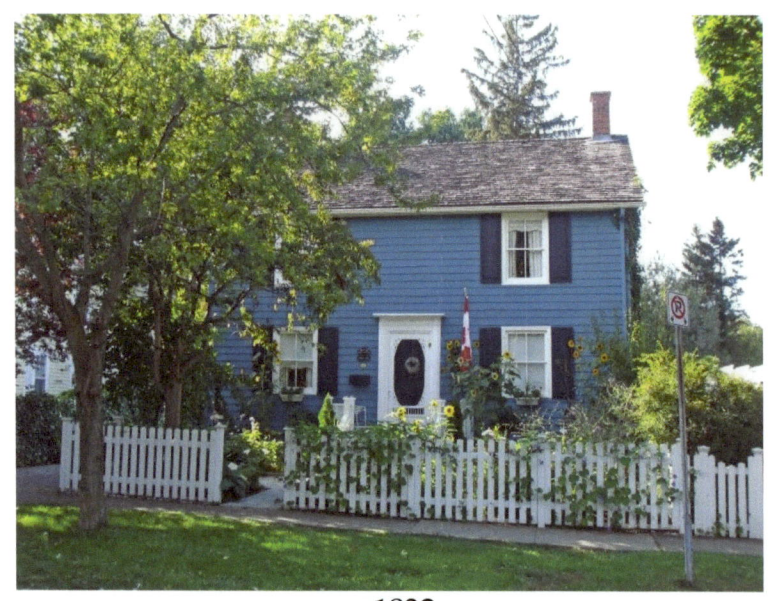

c. 1832

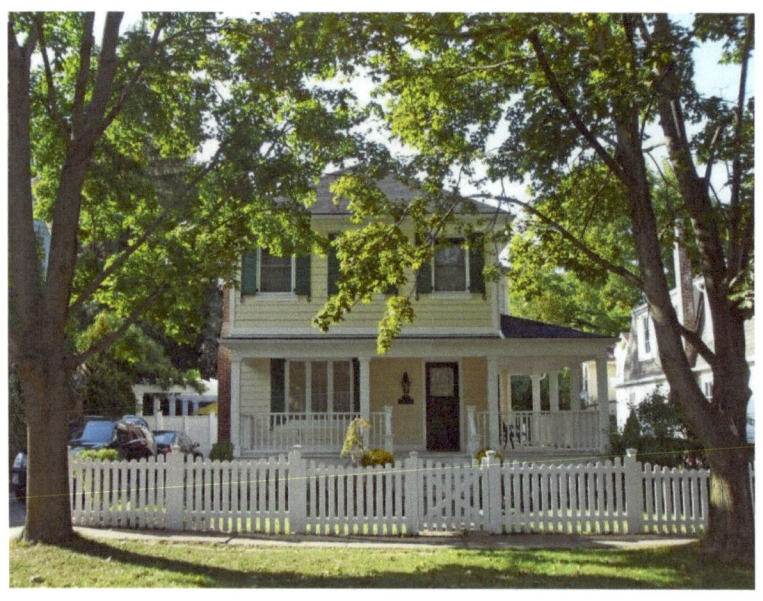

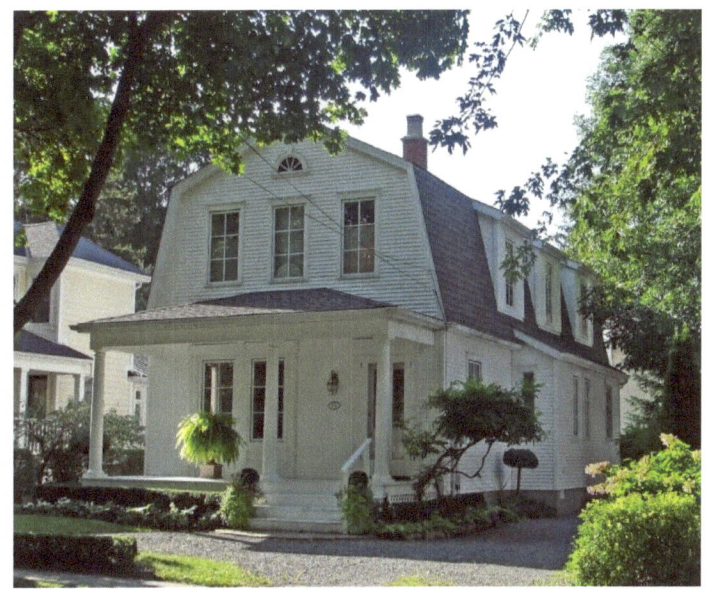

#157

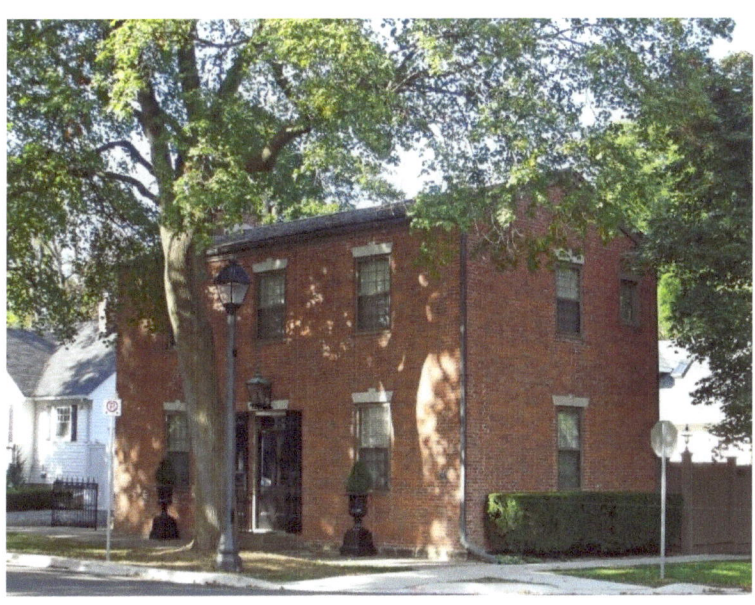

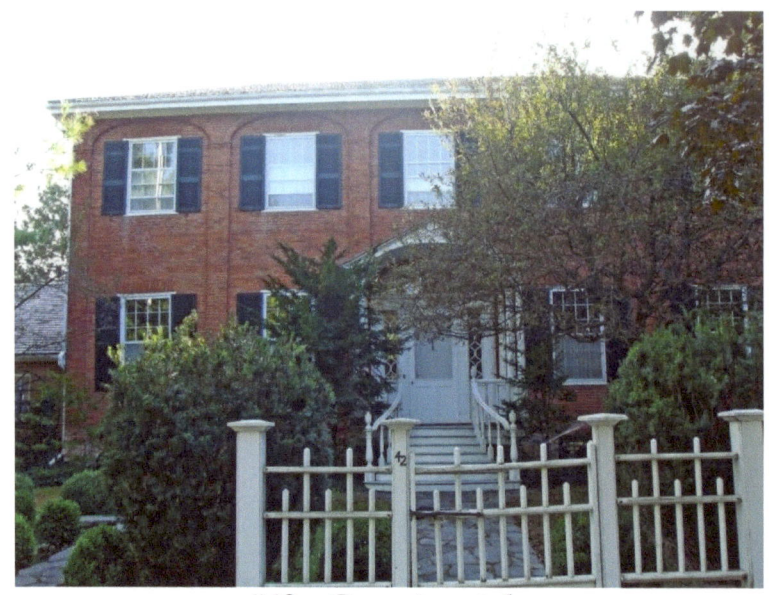

#42 – Georgian style

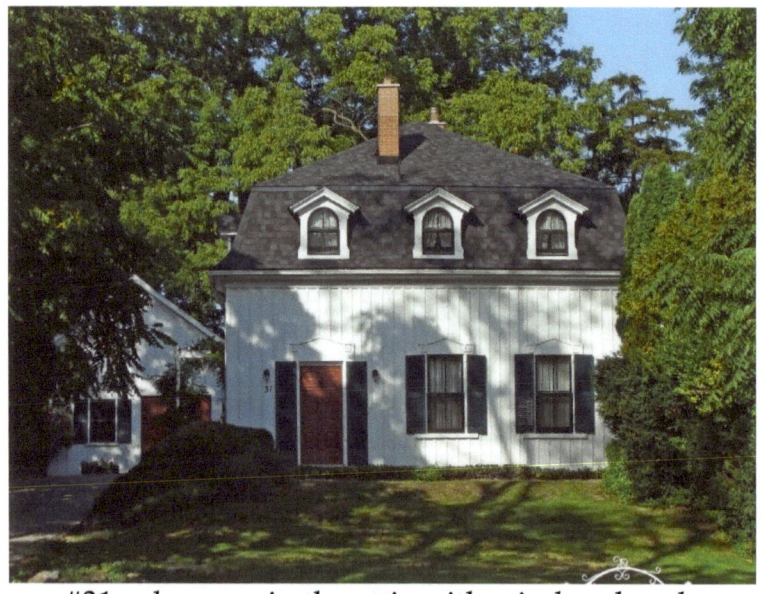

#31 – dormers in the attic with window hoods

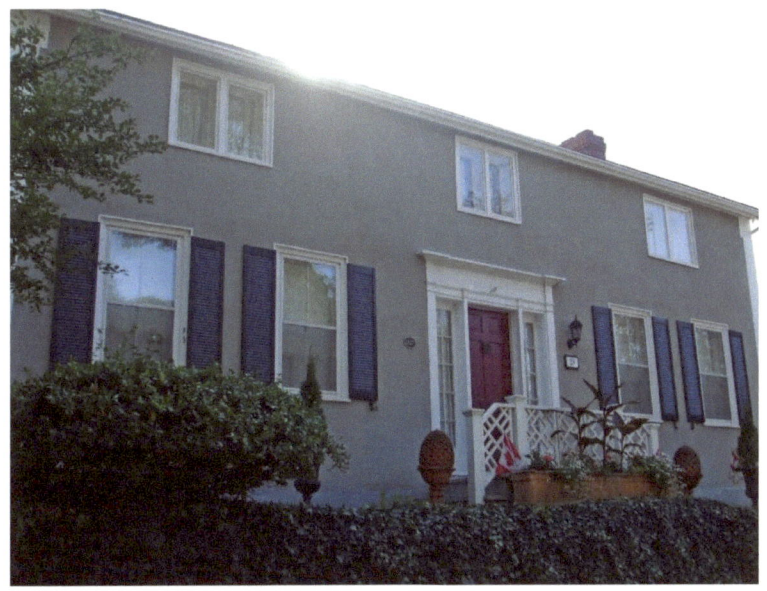

#28 – c. 1817

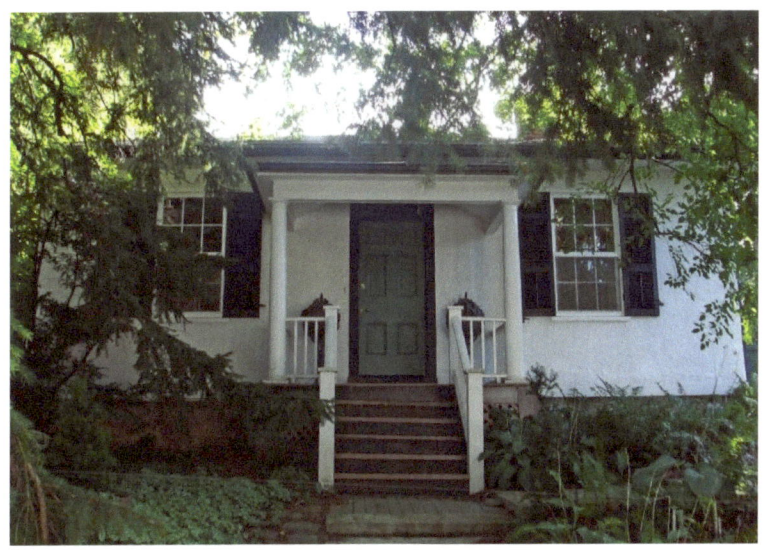

Cottage

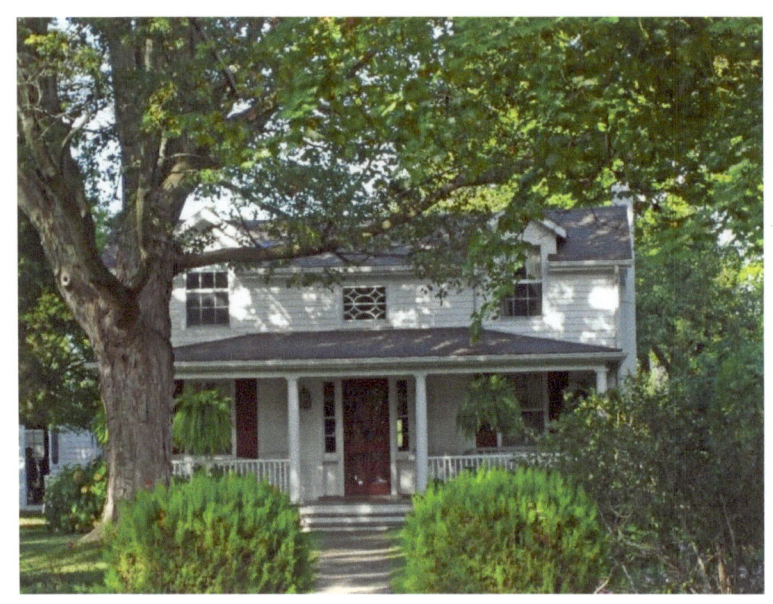

#18

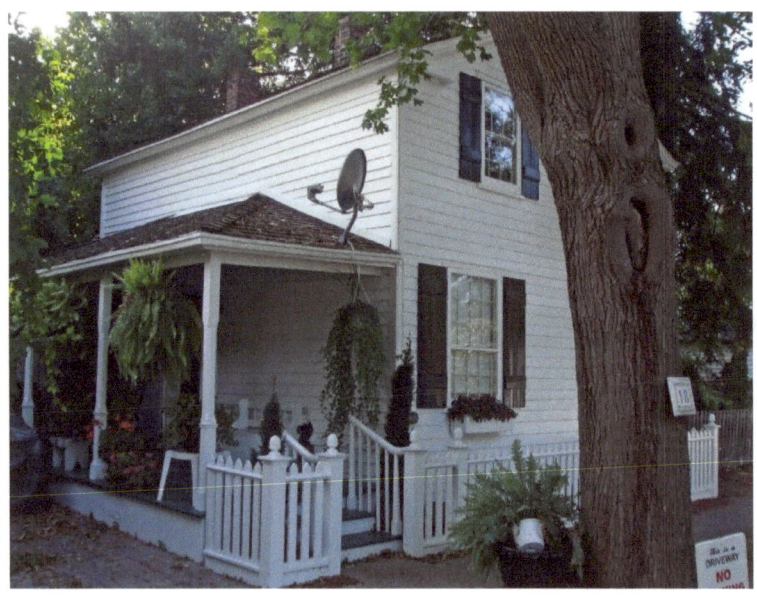

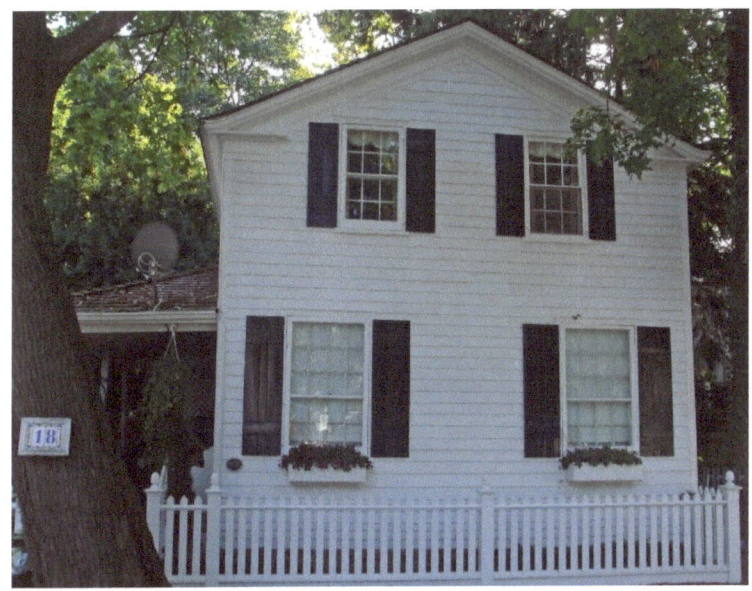

#18

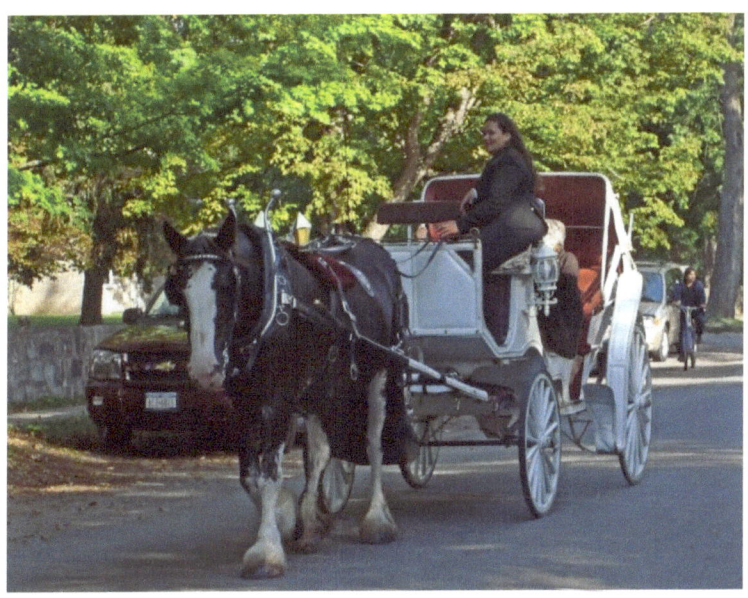

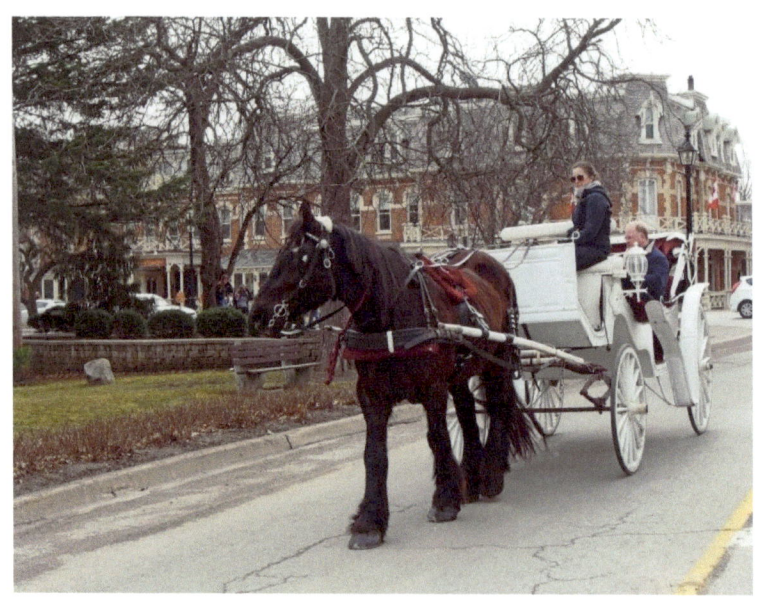

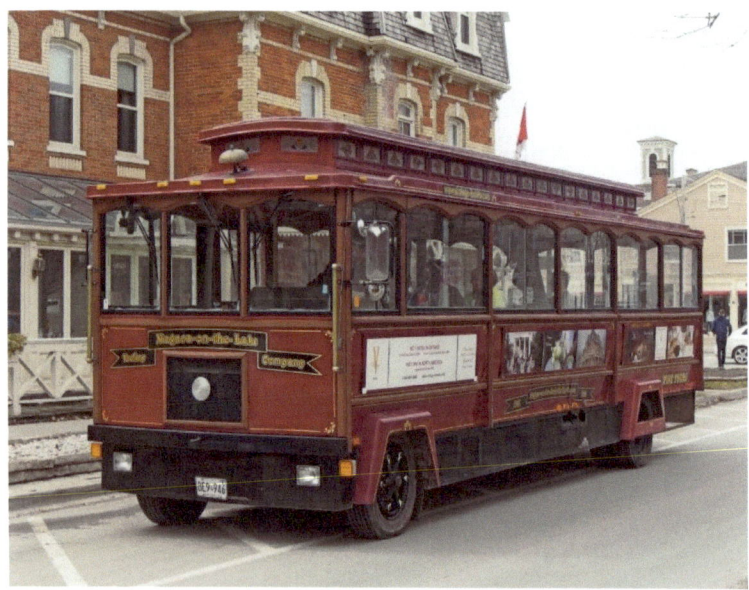

Niagara-on-the-Lake trolley car

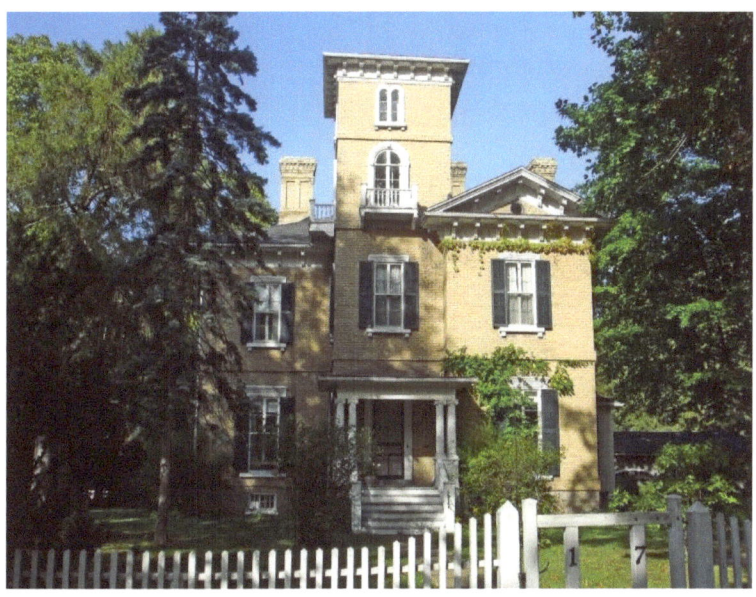

17 Byron Street – Italian Villa style - The upper windows on
the tower have Roman arches; the highest windows are
paired. The cornice brackets are large and ornate. Within the
pediment there is a roundel. The windows on the first and
second storey are rectangular with simple window surrounds
and cornices. Both storeys have elegant shutters. Like many
shutters on older buildings, these would probably have been
working shutters that would close in winter for heat retention.
The portico on the front door is of a Classical design with
Ionic clustered columns and a simple architrave. There is a
discreet string course or band separating the first and second
storeys.

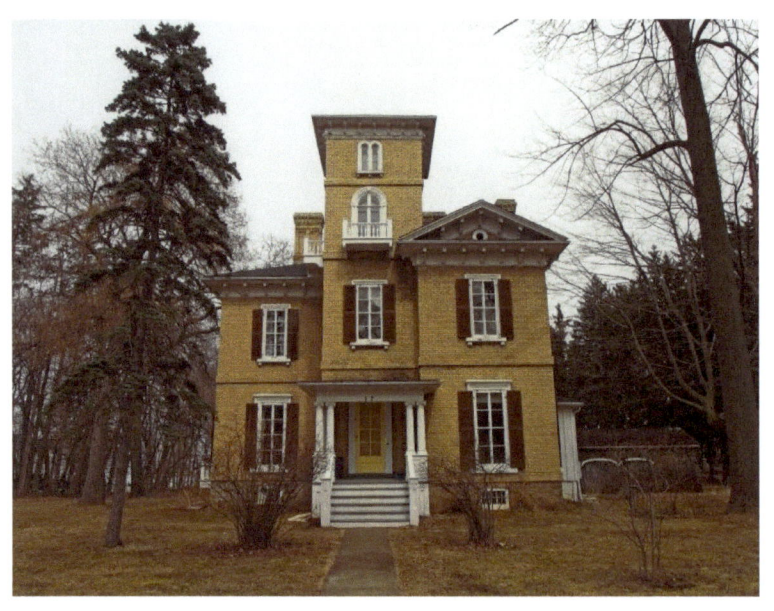

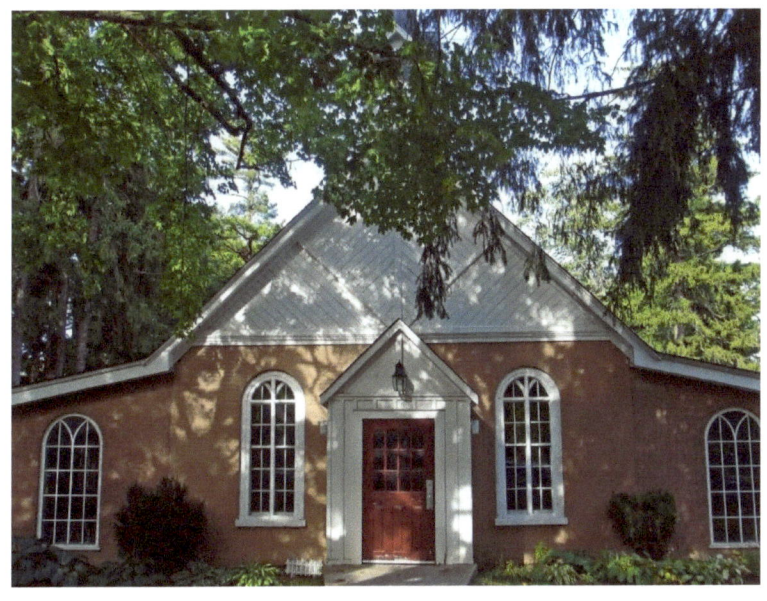

41 Byron Street - St. Mark's Anglican Church Parish Hall

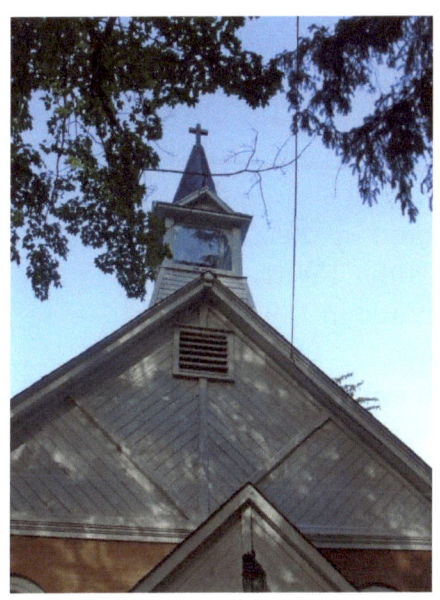

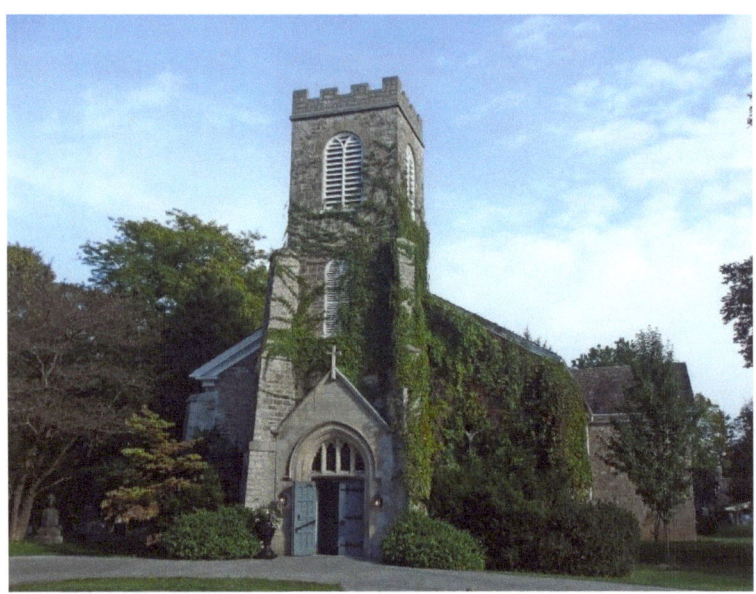

41 Byron Street - St. Mark's Anglican (Episcopal) Church was begun in 1804 to serve a congregation organized twelve years before. Among its early parishioners were Lieutenant-Governor John Simcoe, Lieutenant-Colonel John Butler and Major-General Isaac Brock. Completed in 1810, the building was used by the British as a hospital in 1812 and by the Americans as a barracks in 1813. The Americans burnt the church upon leaving the town. The nave was rebuilt by 1822 and the church was consecrated six years later. In 1843 the structure was altered by the addition of the transepts, chancel, and the present Gothic Revival pulpits. Further interior alterations were made in 1892 and 1964.

Six bells were presented to the church in 1877 by Walter Augustus Dickson and John Geale Dickson in memory of their wives, Catherine and Matilda. Three bells were added in 1917 in memory of Mary Jackes Brown.

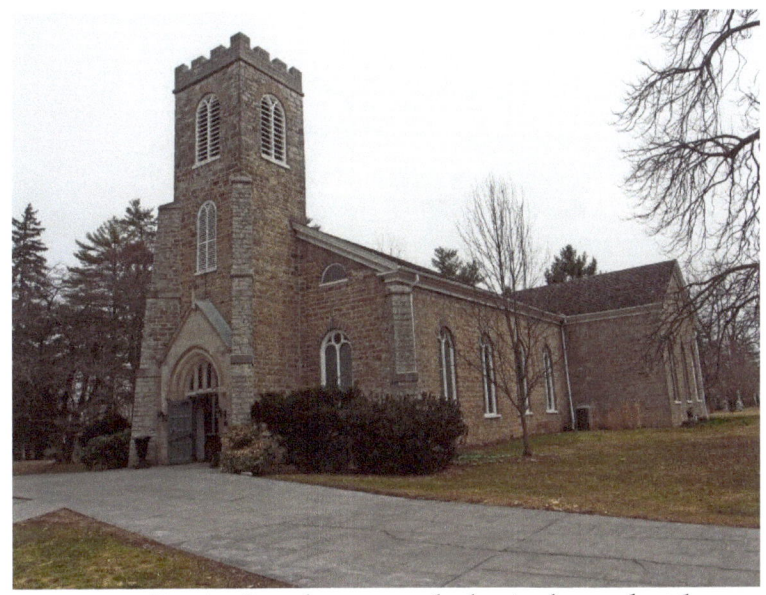

Romanesque Revival style – rounded windows, battlemented
tower, tracery, muntins

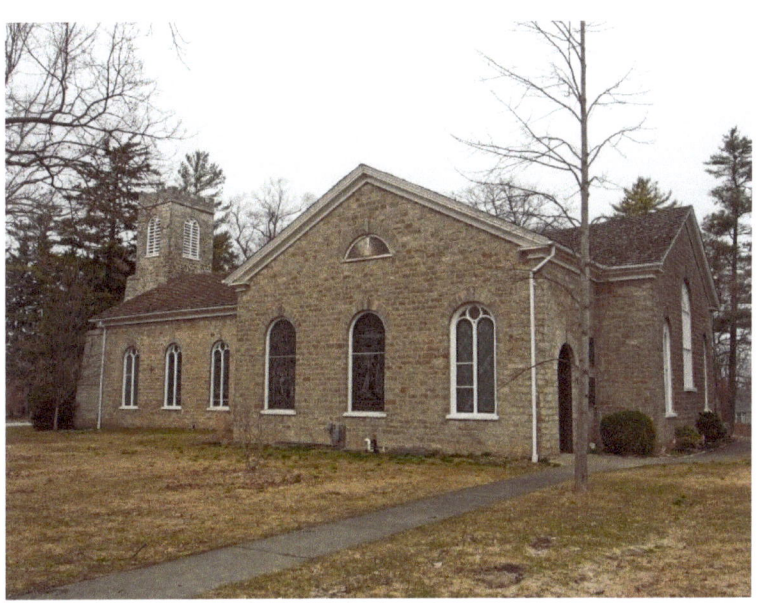

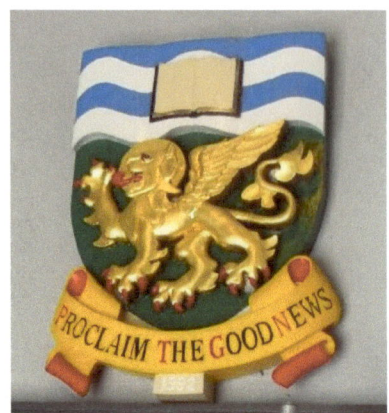

Crafted by parishioner John Hardy to heraldic specifications

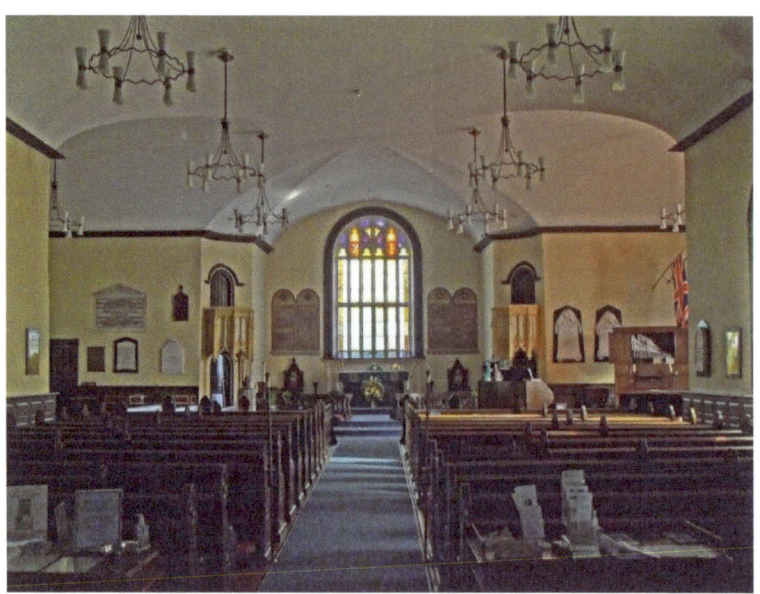

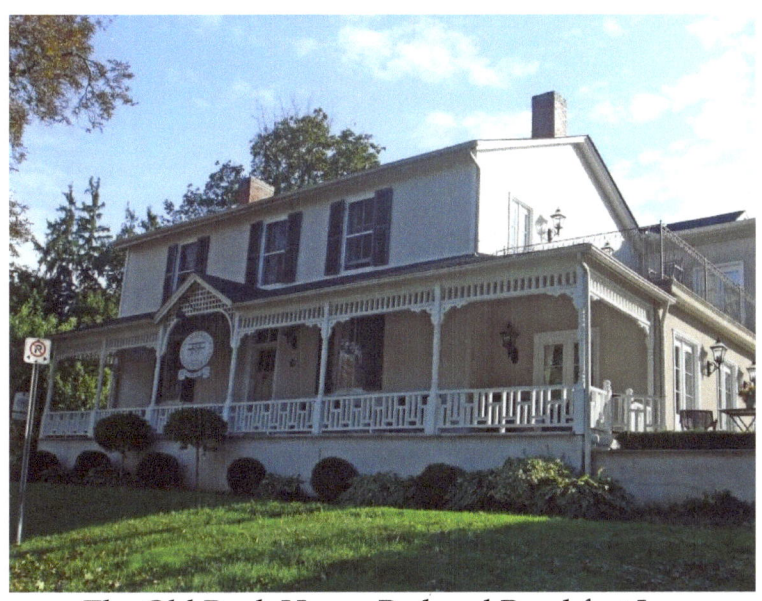

The Old Bank House Bed and Breakfast Inn

10 Front Street

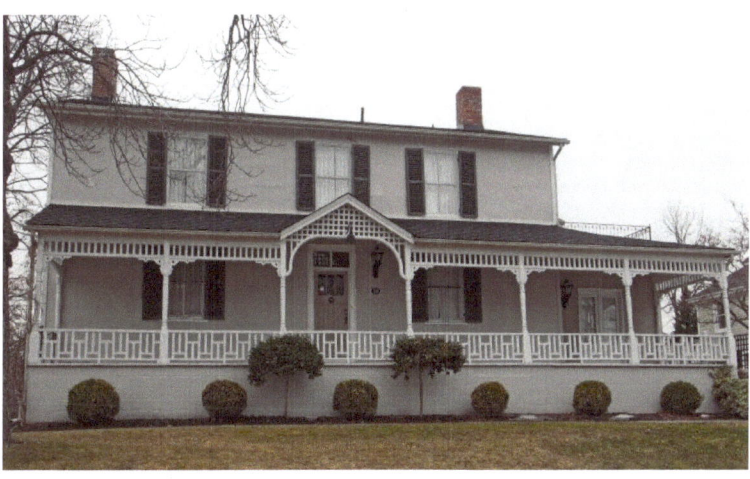

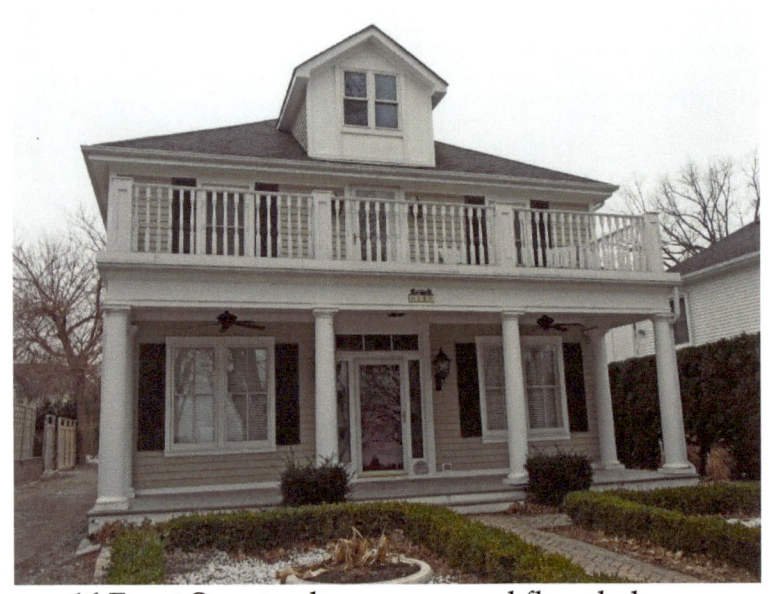

16 Front Street – dormer, second floor balcony

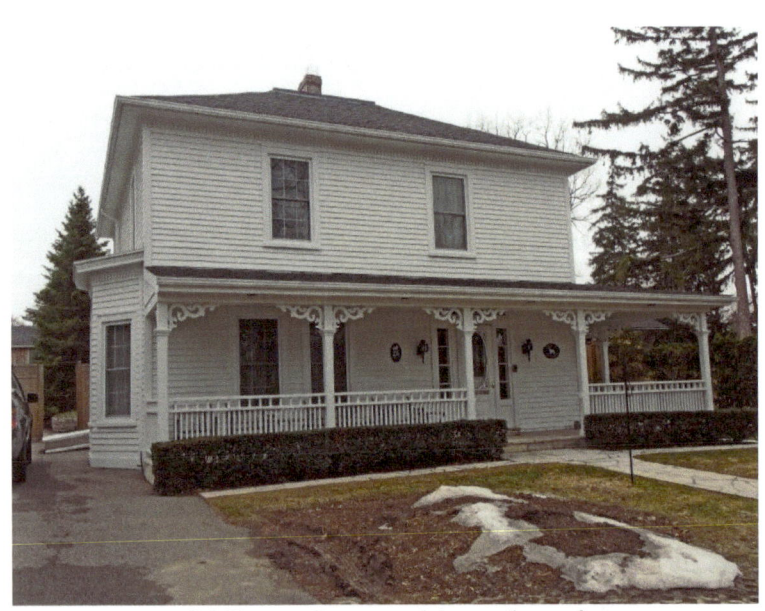

26 Front Street – hipped roof

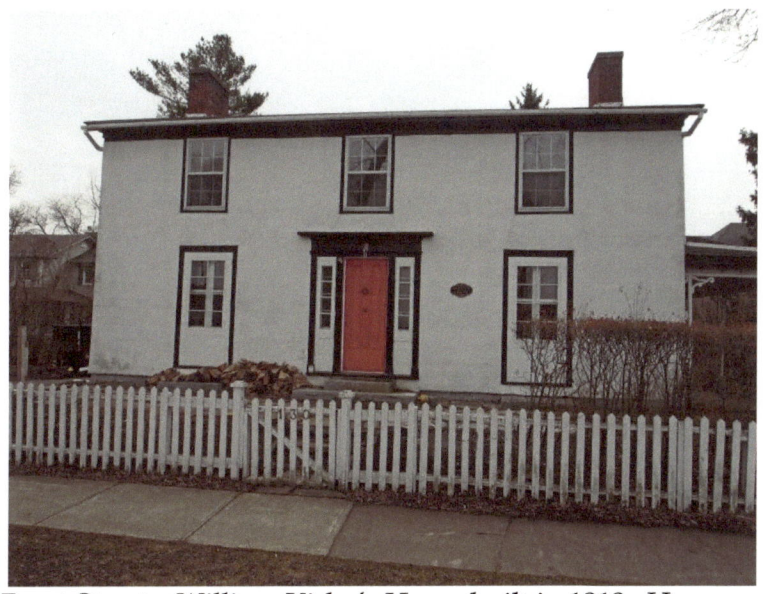

Front Street – William Kirby's Home built in 1818. He was a historian, novelist, poet, and editor of *The Niagara Mail*. His historical romance, *The Golden Dog*, stimulated interest in Canada's history and won him international renown.

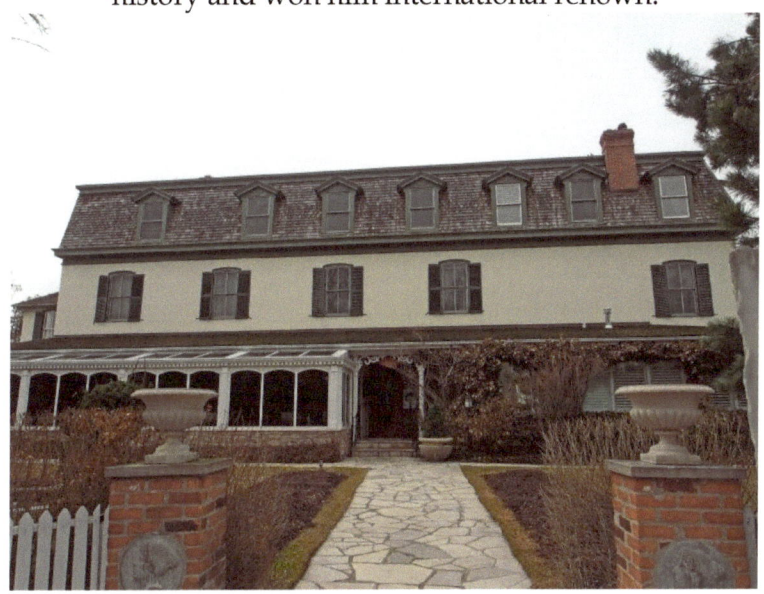

160 Front Street - The Oban Inn – dormers

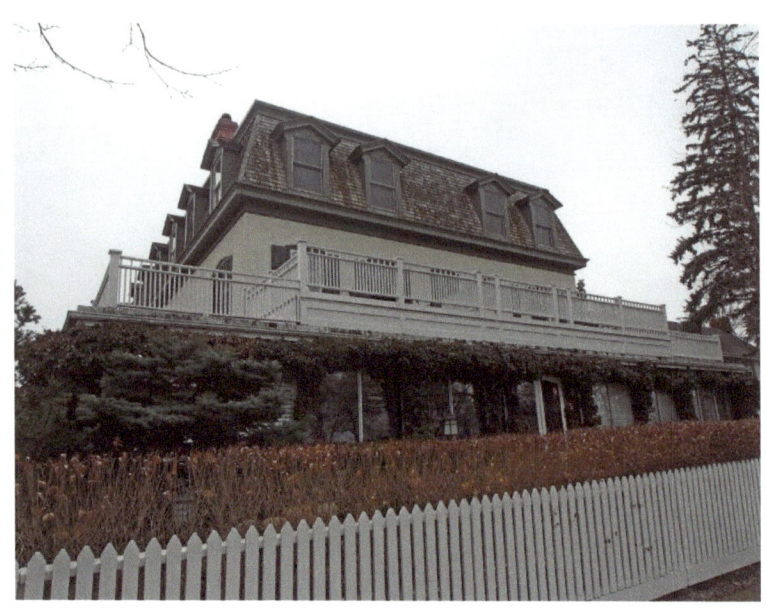

The Oban Inn

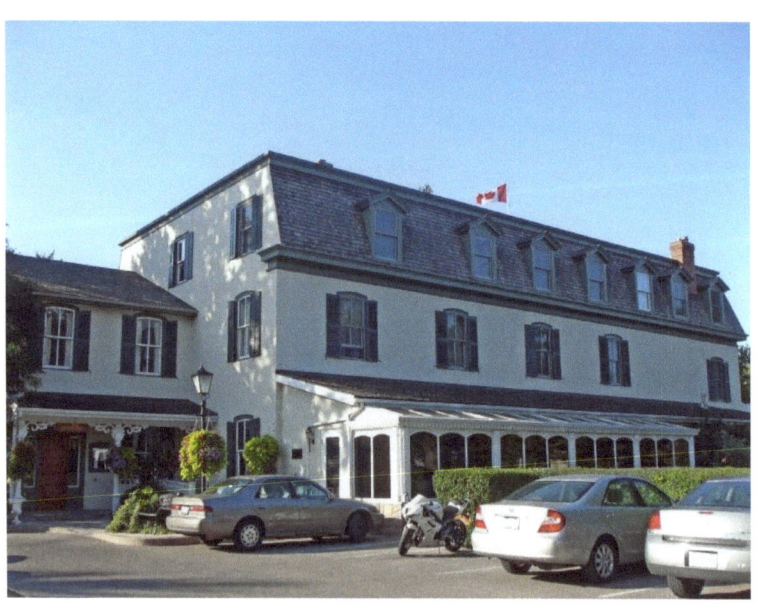

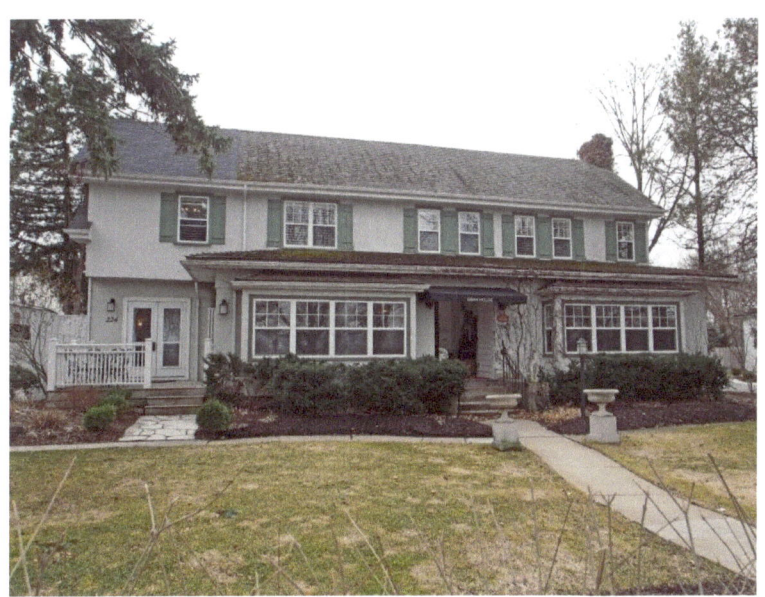

Oban House (#224)

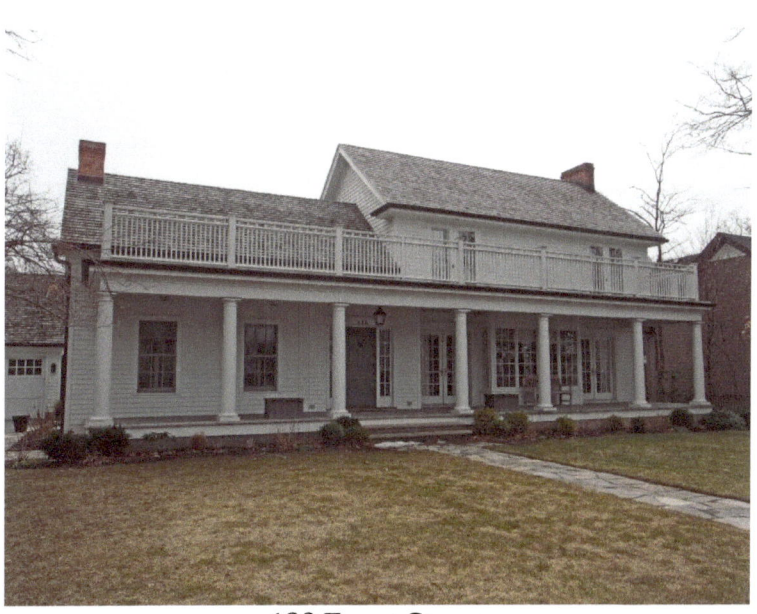

180 Front Street

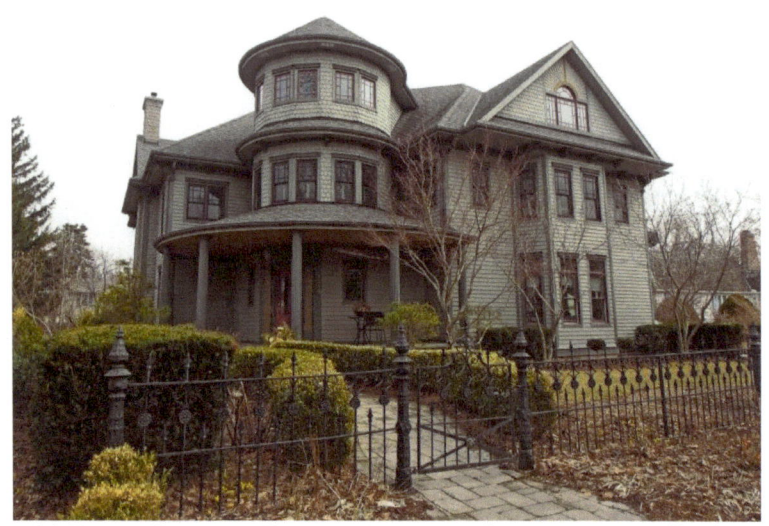

116 Front Street – Queen Anne style – turret, Palladian window

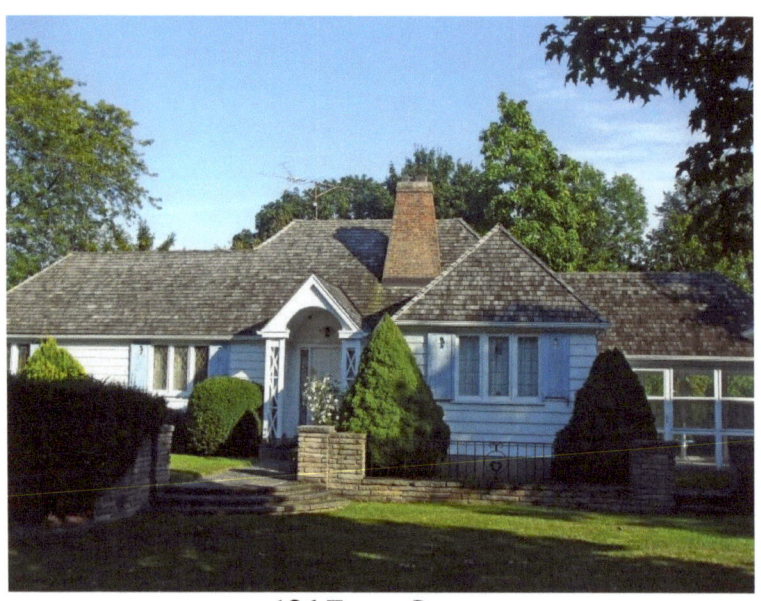

126 Front Street

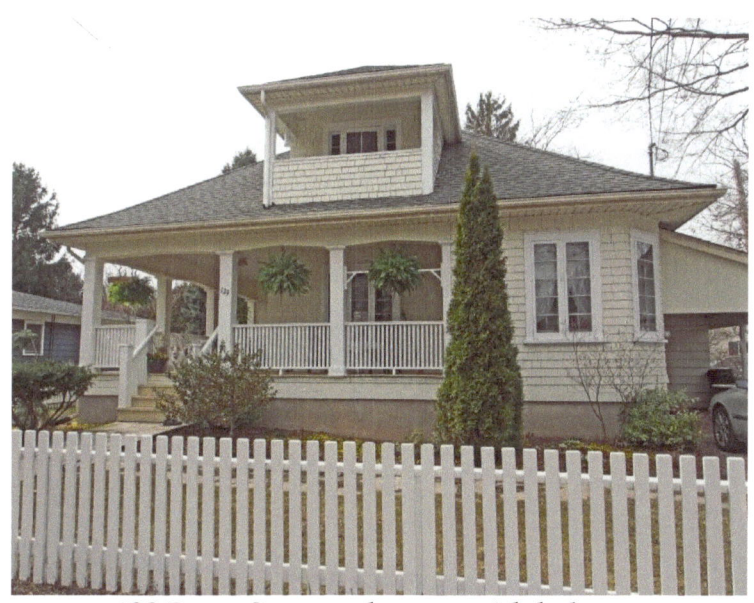

129 Front Street – dormer with balcony

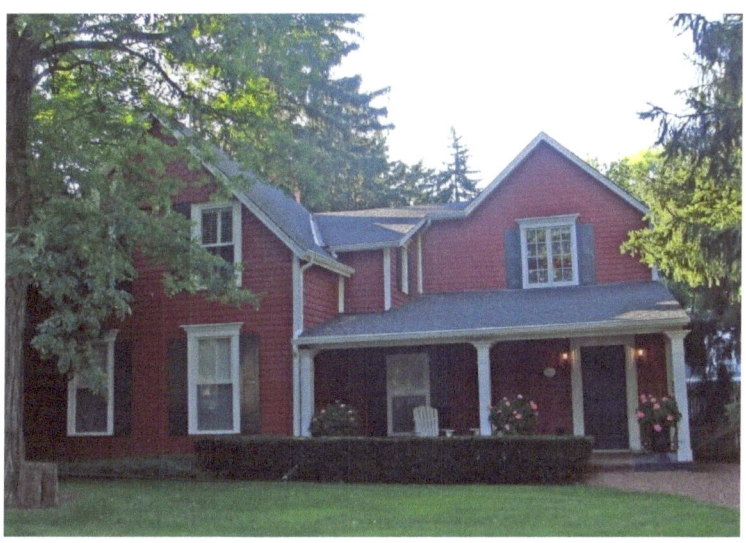

245 Front Street – Gothic Revival

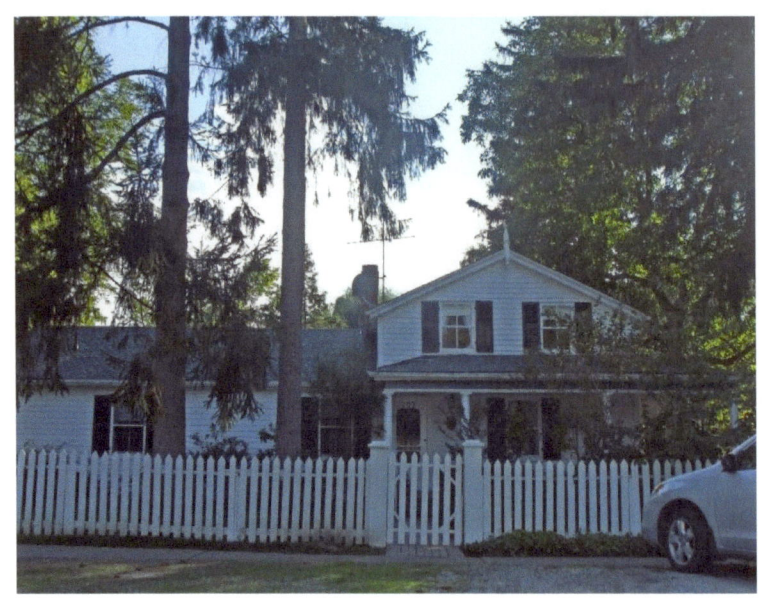

#292 – finial on gable

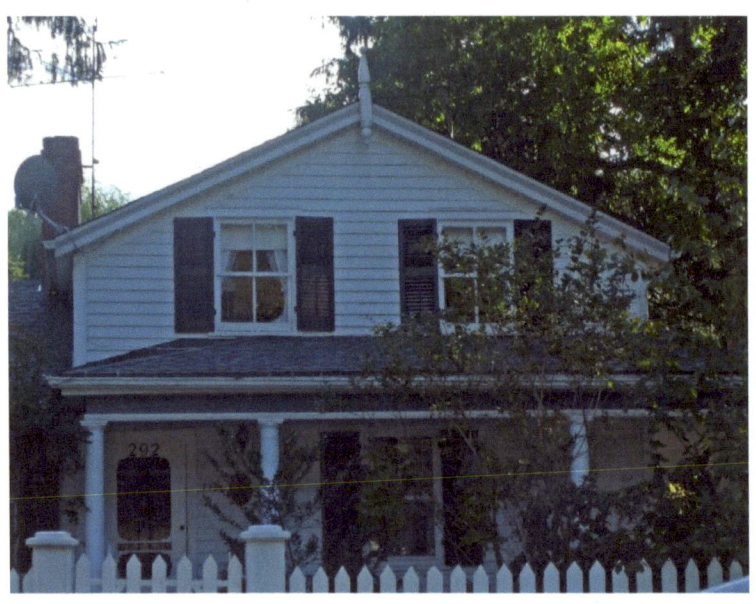

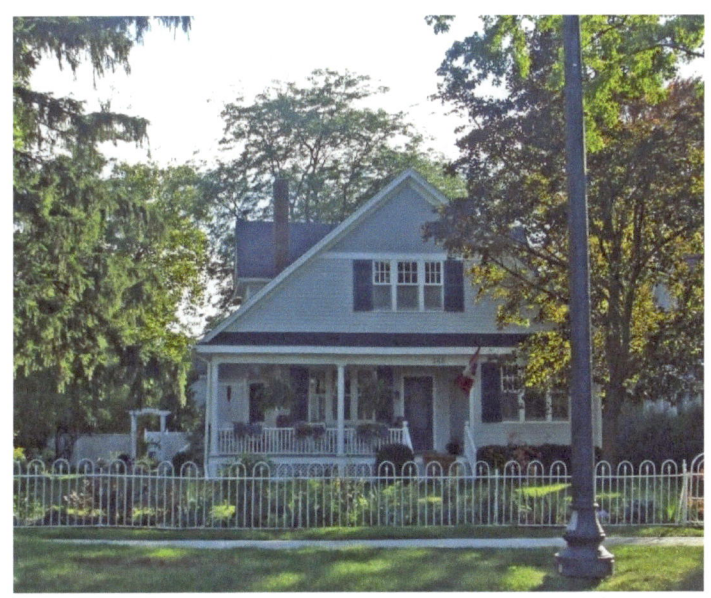

368 Front Street

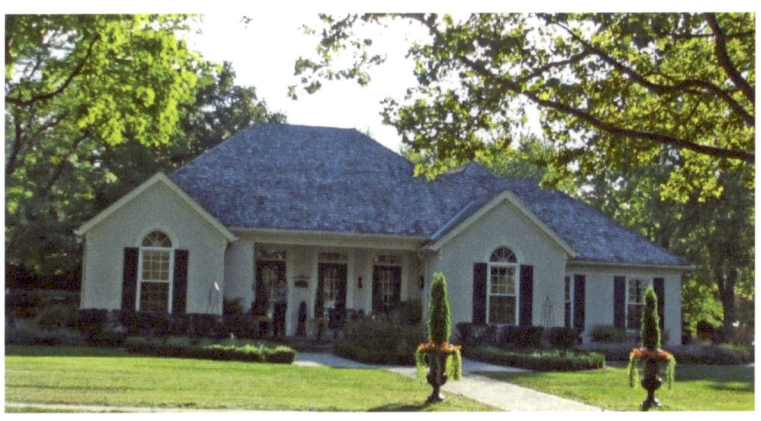

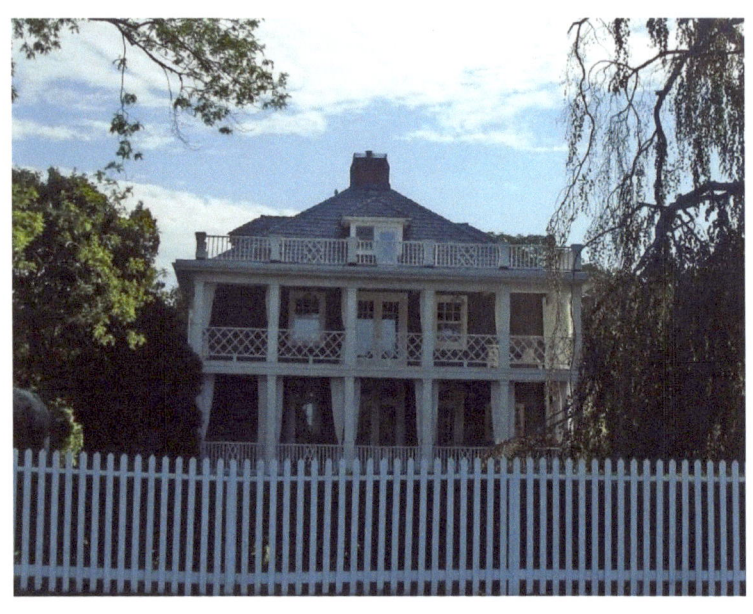

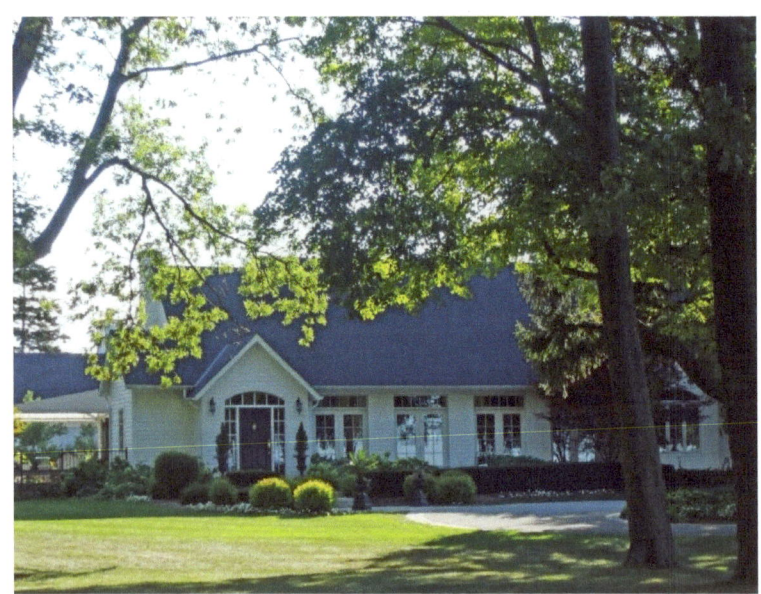

Architectural Terms

Battlement: A design for a parapet that has alternating solid parts and openings, originally used for defense, but later used as a decorative motif. Example: 41 Byron Street, Page 44	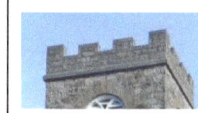
Brackets: a decorative or weight-bearing structural element which forms a right angle with one side against a wall and the other under a projecting surface such as an eave or roof. Example: 9-11 Queen Street, Page 23	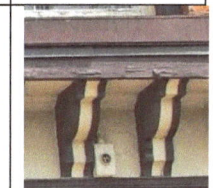
Buttress: a masonry structure built against or projecting from a wall which serves to support or reinforce the wall. In Canadian architecture, they are sometimes used for decoration. Example: 41 Byron Street, Page 44	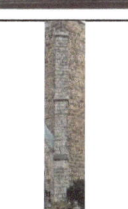
Capital: The uppermost finish or decoration on a column. An Ionic column has a small base, a thin elegant shaft, and a capital composed of volutes which are carved whirls or twists that take the form of a scroll. Example: 17 Byron Street, Page 41	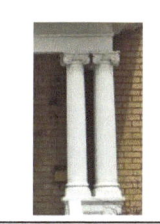
Cornice: originally the wooden overhang of the roof. With the use of stone, brick, iron and steel, the cornice is any projecting shelf at the top of a ceiling or roof. They can be very decorative. Example: 6 Picton Street, Page 6	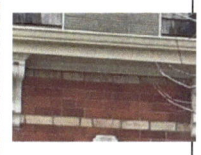
Cornice Return: decorative element on the end of a gable. Example: corner of Queen and Victoria, Page 8	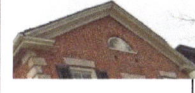

Dentil Moulding: an even series of rectangles used as ornamental decoration in cornices. Example: Queen Street, Page 21	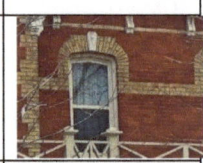
Dichromatic brickwork: the use of two colours of brick, tile or slate to decorate a façade. Example: 6 Picton Street, Page 6	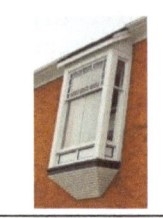
Dormer: (French for "sleep") a gable end window that pierces through the plane of a sloping roof surface to create usable space in the top floor or attic of a building by adding headroom. Example: 54-56 Queen Street, Page 19	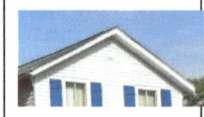
Gable: the triangular portion of a wall between the edges of a sloping roof. Example: see Page 18	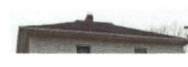
Hipped Roof: a roof where all sides slope downwards to the walls with no gables. Example: 26 Front Street, see Page 47	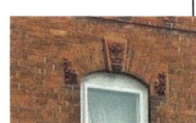
Keystones and Voussoirs: a voussoir is a wedge-shaped element used in building an arch. A keystone is the central stone that locks all the stones into position, allowing the arch to bear weight. A keystone is often enlarged and embellished. Example: see Page 21	

Mansard Roof: This style was popularized by Francois Mansart (1598-1666), an accomplished architect of the French Baroque period and especially fashionable during the Second French Empire (1852-1870). This roof is almost flat on the top section, with two slopes on each of its sides with the lower slope at a steeper angle than the upper and having dormer windows. Example: The Prince of Wales Hotel, Page 6	
Palladian Window: a large window that is divided into three sections with the centre section larger than the two side sections and usually arched. Example: 116 Front Street, Page 52	
Pediment: a triangular section above the horizontal structure (entablature), typically supported by columns. The inside of the triangle is called the tympanum. Example: 17 Byron Street, Page 41	
Pilaster: a slightly projecting column built into or applied to the face of a wall for additional structural support. Example: The Rogers-Blake-Harrison House, Page 11	
Quoin: masonry blocks at the corner of a wall, often a decorative feature, usually larger or of a different colour than the rest of the wall. Example: corner of Queen and Victoria – see Page 8	

Sidelight: a window, usually with a vertical emphasis, that flanks a door, and is often used to emphasize the importance of a primary entrance. Example: 165 Queen Street – see Page 10	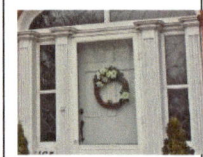
Transom Window: the light above the doorway, also called a fanlight. Example: 165 Queen Street, Page 10	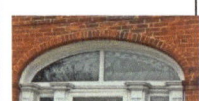
Turret: a small tower that projects from the wall of a building. Example: 116 Front Street, Page 52	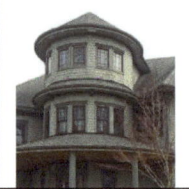
Verge board and Finial: also called bargeboards – hang from the projecting end of a roof and are often elaborately carved and ornamented. **Finial:** ornament added to the top of a gable, pinnacle, canopy or spire – a Gothic element. Example: see Page 53	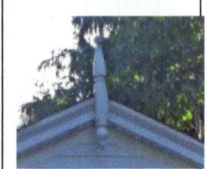
Window Hood: A **hood** is the piece found above window openings, usually of an ornate design, and covers the top third of the opening. Hoods are commonly placed above arched or curved openings on both windows and doors. Example: 6 Picton Street, Page 6	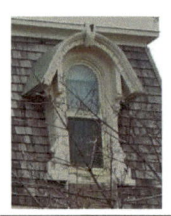

Building Styles

Georgian, before 1860 – This style began with the British King Georges in the 18th century. These buildings have balanced facades around a central door, medium-pitched gable roofs, and small paned windows. Example: 209 Queen Street, Page 7	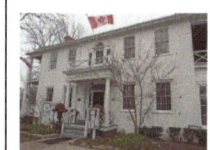
Gothic Revival, 1830-1890 – These decorative buildings have sharply-pitched gables with highly detailed vergeboards, pointed-arch window openings, and dichromatic brickwork. It is a common style in Ontario. Example: 73 Picton Street, Page 31	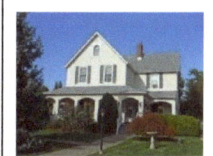
Italianate, 1850-1900 – It has wide-bracketed eaves, belvederes, wrap-around verandahs. Example: 19 Queen Street, Page 22	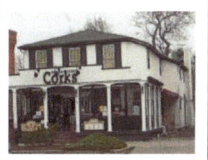
Italian Villa: This style was the first Ontario style that broke from the architectural traditions of the first settlers and imitated the harmony and balance of Classical architecture found in Northern Italian villas. The style is strictly residential and is characterized by an irregular roofline punctuated by a tall tower or campanile (bell tower). Small balconies, cantilevered eaves offering deep summer shade and arcaded porticos are standard features. Architects designing these houses were clearly after the picturesque. Example: 17 Byron Street, Page 41	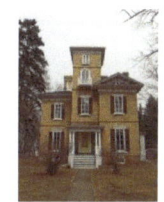

Neo-Classical (1810 - 1850) – This style was a direct result of the War of 1812. Many Upper Canadians returning from the war with the United States were second or third generation Loyalists who had inherited land and means from their forefathers. Once the conflict had passed, they had the money and the time to expand their holdings and indulge their architectural whims. Both residential and commercial buildings were constructed on the traditional Georgian plan, but they had a new gaiety and light-heartedness. Detailing became more refined, delicate, and elegant. Example: 26 Queen Street – Niagara Court House, Page 26	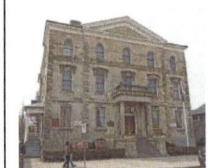
Queen Anne, 1885-1900 – This style is distinguished by an irregular outline featuring a combination of an offset tower, broad gables, projecting two-storey bays, verandahs, multi-sloped roofs, and tall, decorative chimneys. A mixture of brick and wood is common. Windows often have one large single-paned bottom sash and small panes in the upper sash. Example: 116 Front Street, Page 52	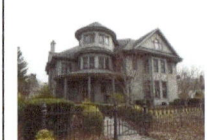
Romanesque Revival, 1880-1910 – This style hearkens back to medieval architecture of the 11th and 12th centuries with a heavy appearance, blocky towers and rounded arches. Example: 165 Queen Street, Page 10	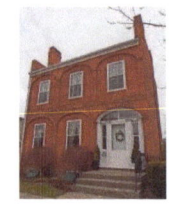

Second Empire, 1860-1880 – The mansard roof is the most noteworthy feature of this style and is evidence of the French origins. Projecting central towers and one or two-storey bays can also be present. Example: The Prince of Wales Hotel, Page 6	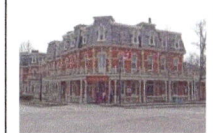
Tudor Revival – exposed timbers with stucco infill, multi-paned windows. Example: 184 Queen Street, Page 9	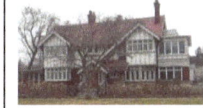